CHALLENGES FACED BY WOMEN

EDUCATION, CAREER AND IDENTITY

SARA HASSAN

BlueRose Publishers

First Published in July 2020

ISBN: 978-93-90223-09-1

BLUEROSE PUBLISHERS

www.bluerosepublishers.com

info@bluerosepublishers.com

+91 8882 898 898

Cover Design:

Mohd Arif

Typographic Design:

Namrata Saini

Distributed by: BlueRose, Amazon, Flipkart, Shopclues

Forward

I am thankful to Research Scholar and Author of this book Ms. Sara Hassan, for her contribution towards women's education and empowerment. Her work reflects the deep hidden pain towards women discrimination and sufferings. Indeed, this topic is the need of today.

I wish her all the best and hope that the readers will surely appreciate her hard work.

Director of Bluerose Publishers

The breeze at dawn has secrets to tell you.
Don't go back to sleep.
You must ask for what you really want .
Don't go back to sleep.
People are going back and forth across.
The door sill where the two worlds touch.
The door is round and open.
Don't go back to sleep.

Jalal Uddin Rumi
13th Century

From the Author's Desk

The purpose of this book is to highlight the importance of education for women, to reflect on the contribution of Muslim women across the world from all walks of life, who struggled for civil rights, environmental justice and equality and also to erase the misconceptions regarding the education of women in Islam.

This is a modest attempt to correct the prejudices about women in Islam and the contribution of women for uplift of society.

A close study of the Importance of women and Contribution of women in general and Muslim women in particular to society has been carried out along with the case study of particular groups. There are many instances of the challenges that women face when they focus on education and attempt to contribute to society.

After a careful and systematic study, the book establishes the truth with examples and illustrations and emphasizes education for women and the challenges they face. It is rather a critical evaluation that enlightens the mind with references from Quran and Hadith to reveal the Philosophy of Education in Islam.

The last few pages of this book are dedicated in honour of the contribution of Indian women in various fields.

My thanks are due to my Professors, Dr. Annie Pothan, Prof. Betty J Gandy Tobin, Dr. Basheer Ahmed, Dr. Ruksana Begum, Dr. Deevena Pauleen and many others for their encouragement.

I am thankful to my husband for his continuous support and valuable words of appreciation. I also thank my family members, friends, colleagues, students, and my children especially for their cooperation and encouragement in publishing this book.

I owe an immense debt of gratitude to my parents for their blessings.

Author

Ms. SARA HASSAN

M.A [English Literature], PGCTE, M.Ed, (PhD-Education)

Contents

INTRODUCTION TO IMPORTANCE OF WOMEN EDUCATION

For a while now, I have questioned myself after observing the society and culture around me - why are we, the women of India, treated as secondary in the family and the community? I am shocked at the injustice that women suffer. I wonder when without a mother, home cannot exist; without daughters, there can't be fragrance at home; without sisters, life cannot be enjoyed to its fullest and obviously, a wife is an essential part of life. Then, why are we looked at as an inferior part of humanity? It is not just with respect to education. It is in every aspect that women cannot lead a life of her own, a life that can give her opportunities, a life which can lead to success and where she can see her dreams come true. Despite many activists, feminists, educationists and philosophers coming forward, only a little impact is seen in the society. Though significant progress is observed around the globe over the years, still there is an area that needs to be improved. With respect to Women's Education, there are extreme examples of patriarchal societies where women continue to suffer, that keep them deprived of education, unlike their male counterparts. The struggle for women education is not over. It is time to get serious about educating women.

Women are undoubtedly the pillars of every family, society and the nation. The importance of women in society has always been tremendous. Women play a very important role in human evolution. Women are an intrinsic part of society. They raise a family, family makes a home, home makes a society and conclusively societies make a country. Women are also pioneers of the nation. Unfortunately, in many cases, women are treated negatively in areas of rights, duties, priorities and freedom in many Indian societies. Even in the modern world, the importance of women in society is undermined very often.

Girls are often denied an education. Without education and empowerment, no development is possible in the family, society and the country. Lack of education restrains prospects, reduces family financial gain, weakens health, sets women and girls under the threat of trafficking and exploitation, increases ignorance and illiteracy in the society and hinders the economic advancement of the whole nation. Education of girls and women is the single most powerful way to advance the lives of individuals, families as well as the economic development of poor communities worldwide. Educated women can help the family and society to conquer many social calamities such as domestic assault, unemployment, dowry system, child marriages, sexual harassment and female feticide. It is only through education that women can influence the family and push the family from darkness to light. Education is a very influential tool that gives society a substantial amount of prosperity which ultimately adds to economic growth, eliminates poverty, lessens crime and strengthens democracy. Education curtails the gap of inequalities between males and females. Educating girls is a way of making sure that they have greater potential to make smarter choices which helps them to lead a successful life. It is a basic human right, not a luxury.

Education means power, but unfortunately in India, it remains largely in male hands. One of the objectives of women education is to make better wives and mothers for the nation. A few communities in our society still fail to understand this and end up making a simple thing extremely complex. One must be informed of the fact that if she is uneducated, then close to half of the population is uneducated. Educating a woman means educating the family and the nation.

Gender discrimination is deep-rooted in India. Thus, we see that many parents from simple families send their male child to school, but not the girl child. It is also a common sight of parents, especially in rural areas, sending their male child to better schools. Even if girls are enrolled, their dropout rate is very high. Why does this discrimination continue to occur even in the present day, one wonders!

Initially, the main activities in women's lives were cooking, being a faithful wife, and then taking care of kids and the household.

Women were not even permitted to vote in the past century. There were very few women educators as women education was and is never encouraged, simply because of the mere fact - women were and are considered inferior to men.

One must be able to figure out the consequences of not educating our girl child. When a woman is not educated, it not only affects her but also the entire family and the nation. In my studies, I learned that illiterate women have high fertility as well as mortality rate because of the lack of awareness regarding the health of mother and infant. It is seen that infant mortality rate lowers to a half in case women have received primary education as compared to illiterate ones. Apart from this, children of illiterate women are generally malnourished. The earning potential of the family is cut down to half when the women are illiterate.

Today, one must think and rethink the importance of women education, which due to patriarchy in our society, is neglected. In witnessing what is going on today, an explosion of reports of misconduct by men of power and sexual abuse have resulted in vanishing the dreams of women who possess incredible skills and abilities. I am a feminist and am in full support of women whose dreams are shattered only because of the patriarchal society. One must understand the consequences of keeping women in clutches of self-made norms, conditions, rules and regulations to lead a normal life as a woman. Patriarchy steals love and affection due to powerful domination. It must be understood that only an educated woman gives due respect, constant support, encouragement, vision and true love to her man and that's how a man becomes successful in his life. She is the one who makes the life of a man beautiful. She is the one who gives him strength. She is the one who helps him make his dreams come true. She is the one who makes him successful.

It is my observation that in Indian society, women have been victims of humiliation, exploitation and torture. Women are a victim of male domination not only in the sphere of educational deprivation but also in the respective fields of life, especially in economic life over decision making on resources and utilization of her individual earnings. In today's world, women with their ambitions, intelligence and strength have proved that they are on par with men.

The word 'excellent' is only appropriate if it is connected with education. Without education, a woman cannot perform her role in whatever place she is standing.

"If we educate a boy, we educate one person; if we educate a girl, we educate a family - and the whole nation."

The research conducted by various organizations has come up with statistical data which sheds light on the current status of girls' education and its impact on families, communities and countries all over the world.

1. 65 million girls all over the world are not in school.
2. The number of primary-school-age girls in the world is 31 million. Out of these, 17 million will probably never attend school in their lives.

3. Currently, there are over 123 million youngsters between ages 15 and 25 who cannot read or write. 61% of them are women.
4. Out of all the children who are in primary school, there are 33 million fewer girls than boys.
5. Females who have a standard 8 years of education are 4 times less likely to get married as children.
6. One extra year of education for a girl means 20% more earning potential as an adult.
7. A baby born to a mother who is literate has 50% more chances of surviving past 5 years of age.
8. Mothers who are educated are twice likely to send their children to school than otherwise.
9. Half of the children who are not in school live in conflict- ridden countries. Girls make up 55% of this total.

Statistical sources: UNESCO Institute of Statistics, Education First, National Academies Press, The World Bank, UNICEF, EFA Global Monitoring Report and United Nations Statistics Division.

This data clearly says that education is one of the main areas of discrimination for women all over the world.

Digging deeper, here are many reasons that state why education is important for women:

- Education initiates high self-esteem and confidence - Successful women believe they have a right to dream and achieve their goals. This also gives them the inner strength to go through hindrances and hurdles with an open mind and seek to learn and grow.
- Education keeps her focused - A stubborn resolve is needed to see ourselves on the other side. When challenging circumstances seek to wreck, the ability to take the next step both effectively and efficiently is required.

- Education builds better social tranquillity - People of different cultures and religions are bound to come together at some point in life. This helps women understand each other better and stay in mutual harmony. Therefore, education can improve social conformity.
- Education generates a positive approach - A positive attitude is a fuel needed to drive an idea from its conception to realization. A positive approach helps make a conscious effort in arresting negative thoughts and replacing them with the positive once. Positive demeanour helps to see the potential that lies within.
- Education helps conquer barriers - Women who have strived in their lives tend to have incredible inner strength. It's at the end of a battle that a better and more valuable person emerges.
- Education builds a strong mind - Strong-minded women exhibit self-confidence, acquire a healthy self-image and take responsibility for their life.
- Education makes a great teacher - Home is the first school and Mother is the first teacher of a child. An educated mother creates a healthy environment for her child to grow and stay safe. It ignites the flame within which can help the child shape the great tomorrow.
- Education creates equality in society - Educating women promotes the idea of equality and liberty. Educated women in the roles of mother, teacher and guardian discard the seeds of inequality and discrimination from the society which finally leads to the development of a nation. Women's sufferings in the name of gender inequality can, to a large extent, be removed by educating women.
- Educating women leads to the development of the nation - Approximately more than 50% of the total population comprises women. Leaving women uneducated will directly hinder the growth and development of the nation.
- Educating women results in an increased number of educated children - Educated women insist on getting their children

especially daughters more educated than them. Educated mothers inspire, motivate, cooperate and support children to get educated and lead prosperous, respectable and successful lives.

- Education of women eliminates poverty and illiteracy from the nation - Women when provided with equal rights and equal access to education participate more in political, economic and business activities, which boost their domestic, social, political, economic and cultural development. Education empowers women by uplifting their earning potentials. According to the United Nations Educational, Scientific and Cultural Organizations known as UNESCO, a single year of primary education has shown to increase a girl's wages later in life by 90%. Illiteracy and poverty are the root causes of all the crimes and violence in the world. This can only be prevented through women education and participation.

- Educated women bring greater economic and social changes - The growing participation of women in politics and decision-making processes promotes a more representative and effective government. Women with leadership skills are a great asset to the nation. Research shows that educated women's participation in politics and their decisions to run the government leads to reduced corruption, less discrimination and a possibility of better decisions which become a major factor in the flourishing economy and social changes.

Hellen Keller said, "Character cannot be developed in ease and quiet. Only through experiences of trial and suffering can the soul be strengthened, vision cleared, ambition inspired and success achieved." Find what is learned in the struggle and it appears to be not as fierce as it appeared to be.

The status of women with self-respect increases with educating girls. An educated woman will be conscious of her rights. She can combat social evils such as domestic violence, dowry demand, sexual abuse, gender discrimination and low wages. Only through education, a woman can be a better human being, a successful mother and a responsible citizen.

My observations and research have reached a point where I believe that every individual is aware of the importance of women education and the consequences of not educating them. However, our traditional and patriarchal system of society does not allow men to dare see their women more educated than them. It is a wrongly held belief that uneducated or less educated women can be more easily controlled and dominated. An educated woman in every role has proved to be reliable, responsible, adjustable and successful. It is high time that society changes its attitude towards women and women education to see a prosperous tomorrow.

~~~~~~~~~~~~~~
~~~~~~~~~~~~~~

WOMEN EDUCATION IN INDIA

Women and girls' Education is a major step towards the success and development of a country. The prosperity of a nation is possible only by Educating women.

India is a Sovereign, Socialist, Secular, Democratic and Republic country. The constitution is a supreme law of India. According to 86th Amendment Article 21, A of the Constitution of India, RTE Act [Right to Education Act] enacted on 4th August 2009 mandated free and compulsory education for children between the age of 6-14 years irrespective of gender. Gender inequality is at its highest level in Indian history. Every page of Indian history cries out discrimination, injustice and inequality not only on the basis of gender but also related to religion, region, community and caste that is against the constitution of India. It continues to be a major barrier for India's development.

Ten years after the Right to Education Act came into being, nearly 40% of adolescent girls in the age group of 15-18 years are still not attending school and 30% of girls from the poorest of families have yet to see a classroom, according to the status report.

According to the report by Right to Education Forum and Centre for Budget Policy Studies with support of the World Bank and UNICEF, poor compliance of RTE – 12.5% across India has been primarily due to the downward trend in financing school education which has come down from 4.14% in 2014-15 to 3.40% in 2019-20.

The RTE Act report also cited that the education and empowerment index is directly related to per child expenditure. Kerala tops the index with an expenditure of Rs. 11,574 per child per year with Bihar at the bottom with an expenditure of just Rs 2,869. Himachal Pradesh, with a spending of Rs 17,921 per child per year, features second among the largest 17 states.

Statistics:

- As per the 2011 census, the women literacy rate in India stands at 65.46% below the world average of 79.7%. [China's is 82.7%]
- The school dropout rate for adolescent girls in India is as high as 63.5%.
- The state with the highest female literacy rate, Kerala, stands at 92.07%.
- Bihar ranks lowest with respect to female literacy with 51.5%.
- There are more than 50 million women in India who neither study nor work.
- Only 27% of Indian women are in the labour force, the second-lowest rate in South Asia after Pakistan.

The report released on the occasion of International Day of Education and National Girl Child Day 2020 stated that while sustainable Development Goals seek to achieve gender equality and empower all women and girls, India is home to millions of 'out of school' children, with girls accounting for a substantial chunk. Pointing concerns over the fact that girls are twice less likely as boys to receive at least four years of schooling. 30% of girls from economically backward groups did not set foot inside a classroom. The literacy rate of women in India is only at 65%.

According to Ambarish Rai, National Convener, RTE Forum, with over 60 million children lacking education in India, insufficient funding for school education has been the bottleneck in achieving benefits under RTE Act "which is an important tool for universalisation of elementary education." The status for girls' education in the country is a matter of grave concern." he said. As per the report, studies have shown a strong correlation between public investment in education and child development and empowerment. The report said that each additional year of schooling's earnings rises by 8% - 10% [with a larger increase for women].

Despite many reforms and strategies taken up by the government of India to promote girls' education, women education has been one of the major issues of concern. After 72 years of Independence, women have to still fight for their basic rights such as education and empowerment. Statistics are not the same for men and women. When it comes to literacy, empowerment and education, there is a bigger gap between the two genders. There are many factors responsible for such a crisis. Due to India's amazing cultural diversity, there are differences in norms, traditions, beliefs, thoughts, ideas and customs from region to region, place to place, one community to another, one society to another and from one religion to another religion. The caste system, family values and patriarchal structure of families are highly respected throughout India and are fundamental in daily life. All these factors have exerted noticeable influence on women and girls' education and empowerment. Women education in India is hampered at every stage.

There are many more reasons which are responsible for hampering women's education. The main reasons for this are crime and violence against women. Crimes like women trafficking, rape, murders and abortion of girl child are a shame for our country.

India has abundant human resources as it is one of the most populous countries in the world. India has the potential to become the human resource capital of the world. It is time to realize that the prosperity of any nation is not possible without the prosperity of women. It is time to erase misconceptions regarding girls and women education.

Currently, the whole world is facing crises so is India. Social distancing, lockdown, sanitization, use of protective gears, isolation and quarantine are the measures to tackle pandemic covid-19 in the absence of vaccine and proper treatment. The seriousness of the problem can only be understood by educated mass. India has witnessed the effects of lockdown clearly different in the areas where people are educated and the places where illiteracy is high. The upcoming months will be a big challenge for the government of India where education, training, health, cleanliness, hygiene and sanitization play important role to overcome covid-19 pandemic. Response shown by educated individuals are satisfactory and prevention from the disease is good when compared to the people from thickly populated and least or uneducated because of their unawareness towards pandemic. Women who are the leaders of homes, communities, societies and the nations have a major key role in preventing their homes and the whole nation from deadly disease. Now the solution is again pointing towards the education of women. Instead of targeting a particular group, religion or community, it must be understood that the illiteracy and ignorance are the only causes of spread. Government must provide with adequate education and training to solve the problem to higher extent. Proper education and understanding is the need of today not discrimination both from the government and citizens.

~~~~~~~~~~~~~~
~~~~~~~~~~~~~~

MISCONCEPTIONS REGARDING WOMEN'S EDUCATION, EMPLOYMENT, FINANCIAL AND LEGAL MATTERS, LOVE AND MARRIAGE, WOMEN IDENTITY AND PATRIARCHY IN ISLAM

Mistruths and misconceptions have been spread about Islam for various reasons: false interpretation of Quranic verses and hadith [sayings of prophet Muhammad (pbuh)], unauthentic sources, personal and national politics, economics, prejudice against the Islamic religion or Muslims in general, hostility towards Islam and Muslims, thoughtless hate, anti-Muslim hate speeches, extremists, stereotypes, biased media or a fear of 'others' (in power).

Islam is one of the world's largest religions. It has principles which are very simple to follow, but unfortunately, this religion is portrayed as a complicated one through different sources. Islam believes in equality, justice, education and empowerment of women. It advocates freedom of conscience, religion and speech. Islam encompasses the universal declaration of human rights. It believes in loyalty to the country of residence. Islam rejects the concepts of violence, cruelty, injustice and hatred.

There are widespread erroneous misconceptions about women in Islam. There are regrettable practices in most Muslim societies where myths, traditions innovations and patriarchy have won over true Islamic teachings where women are traditionally subdued and oppressed.

Women's Education:

It is not true that Muslim women cannot gain knowledge and be educated. Many Quranic verses and Hadith proclaim that regardless of gender, the Quran encourages believers repeatedly to read, to learn, to think, to recite and to contemplate. Indeed, the very first verse of the Quran revealed to Prophet Muhammed (pbuh) was 'READ' and the second revelation speaks about God who teaches people by 'PEN'. In both cases, it is specified to humankind that no gender is indicated. That basic human right of gaining education was supposed to be the right of males is a misconception and can be erased by gaining true knowledge of the Quran and hadith. Many Quranic verses and Hadiths [sayings of Prophet Muhammad (pbuh)] are discussed in detail to prove that women are encouraged to gain knowledge. Islamic history marks many women scholars.

Islam and Quran nowhere restrict women from accomplishing themselves or attaining their goal. No doubt there are many barriers erected by societies only because of patriarchy and dominance of men. Men in the role of husbands in most of Muslim communities tries to keep wives under their feet without due respect. However, every man understands the importance of wife in making his house a home, but does not try to understand woman's will and wish. He Restricts woman from getting her basic rights. Wife is taken granted to give him comfort by every mean. Men with misunderstanding of Islamic teachings, directly or indirectly convey that women's place is under their feet.

Islam forbids men from mistreating women through Quranic teachings and by portraying the life of Prophet Muhammad (pbuh). The Prophet (pbuh) set an example for the treatment of women through his relationship with his wives. He was a great supporter and companion for his first wife Khadija (RA) in her business and also as a husband. Aisha bint Abubakar (RA) was a beloved wife of Prophet Muhammad (pbuh) for her education and intelligence, in particular her ability to read and write. She was often consulted about the teachings of Prophet (pbuh) after his death.

- Quran States, " O Mankind! be careful of your duty to Lord who created its mate and from them twain hath spread abroad a multitude of men and women. Be careful of your duty towards Allah in who ye claim(your rights) of one another." [Quran 4:1]

Employment of Women:

The second-most common misconception regarding women employment is that they are not permitted to leave homes for work or to earn their living. It is also a misconception that Islamic women because of the restrictions of Parda and Hijab are not allowed to work outside the home. And it is wrongly believed that dress code is a big barrier for Muslim women to gain employment and improve their standard of living, though the Islamic history is replete with women who have contributed in every field of life. There is no doubt that Islam encourages every woman to make her house her first priority, but there is no prohibition for women if they wish to work and earn their living with a modest dress code of Islam. Muslim women have been given the privilege to earn money. She can hold a job or run her own business and no one has a claim on her earnings including her husband. Islamic history shows that Muhammad's (pbuh) first wife Khadija was a trading woman who hired Muhammed (pbuh) to work for her. Muslim women took an active part during battles, took care of the wounded and helped in the backline of troops. Contribution of great Muslim women to society are discussed below which gives clarity that women are masters not just in making homes, but for standing hand-in-hand with men to uplift the community too.

Financial and Legal Matters:

Another common misconception regarding the Muslim religion is that Islam keeps women away from financial and legal matters. It is believed wrongly that financial and legal heirs are only male children and daughters have no right to claim their part i.e. daughters and wives are deprived of getting the right in financial and legal parts of their fathers and husbands.

Islam is a religion of equality and justice. It gives equal and specified rights in every aspect to both sexes. Keeping daughters and wives away and not giving them their rights is regarded as a big sin in Islam.

The Quranic verse 4:11, thus establishes the legal entitlement for both men and women in inheritance. A few verses in Surah 4, the apportioning of inheritance is laid out where by sons are stipulated to receive more of their parents' estate than daughters which leaves a misconception that Islamic inheritance law is unfair towards women. This would be however a misunderstanding. Ibn Kathir, a great Islamic Scholar justifies the discrepancies of inheritance between daughters and sons by giving the following explanation; 'Men receive greater shares of inheritance in a system in which they function as a provider for the family, and in which a wife is entitled to the entirety of both her own wealth and husband's wealth and a husband is entitled only to his own.' Thus one must understand that Islam leaves no space for injustice and inequality to exist. According to every school of Islamic Law, the injunctions of the rules of Islam apply to every Muslim who has reached the age of maturity.

Quran states: "for men is a share from what the parents and near relatives leave, and for women is a share from what the parents and near relatives leave from less from it or more, a legal share….."

-[Al-Quran 4:7]

The rules of inheritance are specified by a number of Quranic verses which includes - Surah "Baqarah" (chapter 2) verse 240.

Surah Nisa (chapter 4) verses 7-12, 19, 20 and 33.

Love and Marriage:

It is a misconception about Islam that women have no right to choose their husbands. It is common that girls play a passive role in their own marriages as they must be obedient daughters who follow the wishes of their parents. In fact, no right is given to women to choose their husbands. It is not an Islamic law, but a local, tribal and cultural tradition or custom.

Quran and Islamic rules prohibit extramarital love and sex. Indeed Quran and Hadiths emphasize the importance of love of women (wives). Parents are no doubt instructed to take the consent of their children. A daughter's consent is always sought as the priority in selecting husbands. The truth is that Islam expects marriage to be established on mutual understanding, approval and acceptance.

Marriage in Islam is viewed as a sacred union between a man and woman that fulfills half of the religious obligations. A well known verse from Holy Quran states marriage as: "Among His signs is that he created for you spouses from yourselves so that you might find tranquility with them. And he has placed between you affection and mercy. In that there are certainly signs for people who reflect."[Quran-30:21]

Islam puts strong emphasis on mutual love, respect and understanding between a husband and wife. Marriage is a legal social contract under Islam between a man and woman, not a holy sacrament. At the time of nikah(marriage), bride is asked if she is willing to marry groom, that means she has a choice in this matter. Forced marriages are haram or forbidden in Islam. The terms and conditions of nikah(marriage) clearly mention husband to be kind, respectful, just and affectionate towards his wife, but the misconception regarding marriage in the mind of a husband is that, he regards the contract as for himself the owner of body, mind and soul of his wife. There are many problems a woman has to face when her husband does not fulfill the moral and ethical responsibilities. Repeated negative behavior, verbal and physical violence, economic abuse, mental torture and many more issues are observed in day to day life which lands a woman in stress, depression, anxiety and in many extreme cases suicidal attempts, even though suicide is haram and prohibited in Islamic teachings. Islam promotes the teachings of patience, tolerance and forgiveness at difficult and hard times. When woman finds it miserable to continue life with her partner and does not want to live with him, Divorce and Qulaa are permissible. I have observed women unable to bear continues torture develop negativity towards life and their life partners. The result is the total failure of family life.

Islam condemns all forms of cruelty and abuse; Prophet Muhammad(pbuh) stated,

- "there is to be no harm nor reciprocating of harm."
- "An honorable man treats women with honor and respect, and only a despicable person treats women poorly."
- Prophet Muhammad (pbuh) made a clear pronouncement against domestic violence stating, "Do not strike the female servants of God and do not hit them and do not revile them."

Indeed, the Prophet's (pbuh) emphasied on women's rights in his last sermon, " My parting counsel (wasiyya)to you is to treat women with kindness for verily they are your partners and committed helpers."

He criticized the custom of gender bias in favor of sons and taught, "Treat your children equally when you give gifts. And if I were to favor anyone over another, I would favor women over men."

There are several Hadiths where Prophet Muhammed (pbuh) teaches men to respect, love and care for women. Kindness towards women is the foremost duty of men.

- "You should cherish your woman from the perfume of her hair to the tips of her toe."
- "The best of you is the one who is best to his wife."
- "The whole world is to be enjoyed, but the best thing in the world is a good woman."
- "The most perfect in faith amongst believers is he who is best in manners and kindest to his wife."

Another well-known hadith states that loving conduct and kindness towards one's wife is synonymous with advanced religious understanding.

Women Identity:

It is a wrongly held belief among men that the identity of their women lies with their names. Men regard themselves as our source of Identity.

Many Quranic verses clarify these misconceptions by declaring that her moral and spiritual gains depend solely on her own deeds. Like man, her ultimate failure or success rests on her own beliefs, attitude, behaviour and conduct. Muslim women are equal partners with men in all spheres of life. Thus, Islam gives women an independent identity.

As a Muslim and an Indian, I gained an opportunity to voice my views to eliminate misunderstandings about Islam in this book. It is a well-known fact the women are deprived of due recognition, dignity, respect and honour. Instead, women are given secondary importance in society, with no honour and reward for their dedication and sacrifice. Every contribution of hers is regarded as her duty. The superiority of males lies in their kindness and justice to women. Every person in Islam must learn the true teachings of our Prophet

Muhammed (pbuh), then only is the success and progress of the Muslim community possible. Self-interpretations of Quranic verses and Hadiths must be strictly avoided to learn true Islam. The fallacy has no place in Islamic religion and must be avoided. Learning must be followed by application in everyday life. Islam is a religion of peace, unity, kindness, justice, dignity, and equality. The true essence of the religion lies only with true followers of Islam.

Qur'an states: "And do not wish for that by which Allah has made some of you exceed others. For men is a share of what they have earned, and for women is a share of what they have earned. And ask Allah of his bounty. Indeed Allah is ever, of all things knowing."

(Qur'an 4:32)

The above verse from Qur'an states that 'men shall have a share according to what they have earned and women shall have a share according to what they have earned' seems to mean, to the best of my understanding, that men and women would be answerable to their own deeds, good or evil, that they have earned in using the resources bestowed upon them by Allah.

Patriarchy:

I was doing some research on education for Muslim women, but I could not go ahead without clarifying misconception prevailing to its highest level in the name of patriarchy. This is the root cause of depriving women of their basic rights in every aspect of life, especially in most of our Muslim communities. I cannot restrict myself to just the importance of education for women without discussing patriarchy.

The Quran revealed over 1,400 years ago, confirms the spiritual equality of women and men, gives women the right to inherit, to own property, to seek a livelihood, the right to express their thoughts, the right to give opinions, to marry only by their consent, to divorce if circumstances are not comfortable and to be educated.

Overcoming patriarchy requires us to remember a few things about our religion: The revelation from God applies to men and women equally. Both men and women will be held accountable equally in and hereafter. In the vision of Islam, both men and women are inherently equal in their nature and relation to God and deserve equal dignity. Allah always commands justice. Injustice to womankind has no place in Islam. A true Muslim, who understands this should, therefore, be among those who do not deprive women of their right, dignity and respect.

To justify the position of women in Islam, here are a few quotes from the Holy Quran and Hadiths depicting women's equality to men and their status in Islam.

- Holy Quran says - "and for women are rights over men similar to those of men over women......" *[Quran, 2:228]*
- "And among God's signs is this: He created for you mates from among yourself (males for females and vice versa) and that you might find tranquillity and peace in them. He has put love and kindness among you. Herein surely are signs for those who reflect." *[Quran, 30:21]*
- Their lord responded to them: "I never fail to reward any worker among you for any work you do, be you male or female - you are of one another.." *[Quran, 3:195]*
- "They (your wives) are your garments and you are garments to them..." *[Quran, 2:187]*
- "The believers, men and women, are helpers, supporters, friends, and protectors of one another, they enjoin all that is good, and forbid all that is evil..." *[Quran, 9:71]*
- "Observe your duty to Allah in respect to the women, and treat them well." *[Prophet Muhammed's (pbuh) last sermon]*

~~~~~~~~~~~~~~
~~~~~~~~~~~~~~

WOMEN'S EDUCATION IN ISLAM

Islam gives basic preference to knowledge, its acquisition and application. It is regarded as the fundamental element for all Muslims to believe, think and act according to the principles of the religion. However, discrepancies in styles of interpretation of the Quran have led to the text being translated against its own fundamental worldview. Based on the study of selected Quranic verses, Hadiths (sayings of Prophet Mohammed (Pbuh), one will discover the importance of gaining knowledge of different kinds to achieve divine requirements as well as all forms of human endeavour. According to the teaching of Islam, education is of foremost importance.

The first revealed word of the Quran commanded the believers to "Read!"

This command didn't distinguish between male and female believers. If you have heard that Islam suppresses the women, it is false.

Back in history, 1,400 years ago, Islam gave women the authority to own and dispose of property and earnings without any guardianship over hers, the right to be educated, to go out for work, to choose their husbands, to keep their own family names, and to inherit property.

There is a widely held misconception that Muslim women are considered inferior to men. That they are oppressed because of the way they dress and are denied basic rights. In fact, Islam has granted women the right to inherit, trade, invest, seek financial gain, own, buy and sell assets, seek knowledge and education.

In contrast, the west has granted women only some of these rights in recent decades.

In the words of Prophet Muhammad (Pbuh) - "Seeking knowledge is Obligatory upon every Muslim."

Irrespective of age, gender or colour, acquisition of knowledge and recognition are some of the basic rights of a woman for which she never has to ask, demand or fight. These rights have been granted to her by Allah (God) himself.

Former to the revelation of the Quran, women in Arabia and beyond were treated as slaves and denied their independence and rights. Even in some western countries, women were considered wicked or as witches and associates of the devils. Women have been victims of ruthless power. This superiority over women has been executed in the form of Sati, Hitobashire, Karo-Kari and the killing of witches, which are only a few to mention. Sadly, but truly many societies continue to exhibit this authority in different forms such as failure to educate women, unequal salaries in workplaces, forced marriages, ill-treatment by husbands and prostitution among many others. Not only was the birth of a daughter in any family regarded as a great misfortune, shame and indignity by cruel fathers, but also the tradition or habit of killing baby girls and burying them alive was widespread. As an adult, she was a sex object who could be bought, sold and inherited. Thus, a woman was regarded as a threat to family honour and dignity.

Prophet Muhammad (Pbuh) came at a time when the Arab society, like so many patriarchal communities, was prevalent with repulsive practices against girls. Muhammad (pbuh) preached Islam, liberating women and girls in every walk of life, giving rights to women, respect to womenkind and educating females - all this being a prime aspect in true Islamic teachings. His life portrayed the example of himself as a kind, loving husband and an affectionate father. Thus, Islam has been a special blessing for women. Islam elevated the position and treated a woman on an equal footing with man, and in some cases, even gave clear precedence over man. Once, a man asked Prophet Muhammad (pbuh) - "Who deserves the best treatment from my side?" To this, the Prophet (pbuh) replied thrice, "Your mother." Then, the man asked, "Who is next?" Prophet Muhammad replied, "Your father." At another instance, a man came to the Prophet (pbuh) and expressed his desire to take part in a battle. The Prophet (pbuh) asked him if he had a mother. When he answered that he did, the Prophet Muhammad (pbuh) said, "Stay with her, for Paradise is at her feet."

This research emphasizes the status and importance of women's education in Islam. It does so through referring verses of Quran, (Islam's Holy Book) and Hadiths (authentic sayings of the Prophet Muhammad (Pbuh)) along with a brief study on the lives of Prophet Muhammad's (pbuh) wives, His companions, great Muslim women, and the achievements of women in general.

The first Quranic revelation upon our Prophet Muhammad (pbuh) is the commandment to "Read" which lays emphasis on the importance of Education. The importance and acquisition of knowledge have been highlighted more than five hundred times in the Holy Quran.

Let us quote the first Quranic revelation:

- "Read in the name of your Lord who created, created man from a clinging form. Read! Your Lord is the Most Generous, who taught by means of pen; taught man what he did not know." - *(Quran 96:1-5)*

The above verses address "humankind" which includes both males and females to seek knowledge and be more involved in critical thinking. The emphasis is made on the acquisition of knowledge, and expel any statement or action that denies girls or women their right to education.

- Almighty Allah says: "Likewise, We have sent you (our Messenger (pbuh)) from amongst yourselves who recites to you Our Revelations and purifies and sanctifies and teaches you the Book and inculcates in you logic and wisdom and enlightens you which you did not know." *(al- Baqara, 2:151)*

The above verse proves that the prophetic responsibilities of Prophet Muhammad (pbuh) include a recital of the verses, the enlightenment of self, learning and understanding of the holy book, gaining wisdom and communication of the knowledge irrespective of gender.

- The Holy Quran also states, "Can those who have knowledge and those who do not be alike? So only the wise do receive the admonition." *(- Zumar, 39:9)*

The above verse clearly reveals the superiority of a learned person over an unlearned irrespective of gender.

- The Noble Quran specifies "And those who bring the truth and believe there in such are the dutiful." *[Qur'an, 39:33]*
- The Holy Quran teaches every Muslim Man and every Muslim woman to supplicate;

"My Lord, Enrich me with knowledge." *[Qur'an, 20:114]*

- Allah says in another verse in Qur'an, - "so only those of His servants who have knowledge fear Him. Surely, Allah is Almighty, Most forgiving." *(Fatir, 35:28)*

The above verses signify the importance of knowledge irrespective of one's gender. The pursuit of knowledge and the use of reason, based on sense and observation is made obligatory to all believers.

- In yet another verse in Qur'an, Allah says – "This is a book (the Qur'an) which has sent down to you,(O Muhammad) full of blessings that may ponder over its verses, and that men of understanding may remember……" (Qur'an, *(38:29))*

It is important to remember that the word 'men' in the above verse refers to humankind as it does so in several other places in Quran when Allah addresses humanity. These verses instruct believers that engaging in critical thinking is a moral obligation for both men and women. The Qur'an repetitively reminds people to ponder, think and analyze this using their mind power to contemplate and understand, whilst making no distinction between men and women.

The entire chapter of the Quran is dedicated to women (Surah Nisa). Many verses refer to the treatment and rights of women, such as:

- "'O' You who believe! You are forbidden to inherit women against their will, and You should not treat them with harshness… " *(Qur'an 4:19)*

Similarly, men in their different roles as fathers, brothers, and husbands have a duty to care for women. This includes being financially responsible for them, providing them with basic necessities of life like food, clothing and shelter, supporting their education and protecting them from any harm.

Another verse in the Holy Quran was revealed when the Prophet Muhammad (pbuh) was questioned about the importance of women in the Quran,

- "Verily, the Muslims men and women, the believers men and women, the men and the women who are obedient (to Allah), the men and women who are truthful, the men and the women who are patient, the men and the women who are humble, the men and the women who give *sadaqat* (*zakat* and alms), the men and the women who observe fast, the men and the women who guard their chastity (from illegal sexual acts) and the men and the women who remember Allah much with their heart and their tongues, Allah has prepared for them forgiveness and a great reward (Paradise)." *[Noble Quran 33:35]*

The above verse signifies the equality of men and women in every act, irrespective of their gender in obedience to Allah, truthfulness, patience, humbleness, charity, chastity, and remembrance of Allah and the equality of reward that is Paradise for good deeds.

Let us now examine some Hadiths, authentic sayings of the Prophet Muhammad (Pbuh).

- "Acquisition of knowledge is binding on all Muslims male and female."
- "Seek knowledge, from the cradle to the grave."
- "Acquire knowledge, even if you have to go to China for it."
- "The person who goes forth in search of knowledge is striving hard in the way of Allah, until he or she returns."
- "Whoever teaches some knowledge will have the reward of the one who acts upon it, without that detracting from his reward in the slightest."
- "Allah Almighty makes the path easier for him who walks on it for getting knowledge."
- "Seeking knowledge is mandatory for every Muslim."
- "The best things that a man can leave behind are three: A righteous son who will supplicate for him, ongoing charity whose reward will reach him, and knowledge which is acted upon after his death."
- "He who has a girl and teaches her good manners, gives her education, ethics and then gets her married will be rewarded."
- "The best form of worship is the pursuit of knowledge."
- "There is no man who memorizes knowledge then conceals it, but he will be brought forth on the day of resurrection bridled with chains of fire."

- "Whoever is asked about knowledge that he has and he conceals it, will be bridled on the day of Resurrection with reins of fire."
- "If anyone travels on a road in search of knowledge, Allah will cause him to travel on one of the roads of Paradise. The angels will lower their wings in their great pleasure with one who seeks knowledge, the inhabitants of the heavens and the earth and the fish in the deep waters will ask forgiveness for the learned man. The superiority of the learned man over the unlearned is like that of the moon, on the night when it is full, over the rest of the stars. The learned are the heirs of the Prophets, and the Prophets, have neither dirham nor dinar, leaving only knowledge, and he who takes an abundant portion."
- According to Hadith, "The most complete believer in faith is the best in morals and the best among you is the one who is best to their women." - Prophet Muhammad (Pbuh)

It was narrated that Abu Hurairah said, "the supplications that the Prophet Muhammad (pbuh) used to say for the knowledge were:

» [O Allah, I seek refuge with you from knowledge that is of no benefit, from the supplication that is not heard, from a heart that does not fear [You], and from a soul that is not satisfied."]

» ["O Allah, benefit me that which you have taught me, and teach me that which will benefit me."]

» (Sunan Ibn-e-Majah, Book of Sunnah, Hadith no. 250, 251 classified as Sahih by Allama Albani)

» The Dua of Angels: "Glory to be thee! We have no knowledge, but that which you Thou hast taught us; surely thou art the knowledge, the wise……." *[Surah Al Baqarah 2:32]*

» The Dua of Prophet Musa, "O my Lord! Expand my breast for me, And make my affair easy for me, And lose the knot for my tongue [that] they may understand my word." *[Surah Taha 20:25- 28]*

» Dua taught by Allah, "O my Lord! Increase me in my knowledge." *[Surah Taha 20: 114]*

Prophet Muhammad (Pbuh) praised the women of Madinah for their pursuit of knowledge,

"How splendid were the women of Ansar, shame did not prevent them from becoming learned in the faith."

A detailed study of the life of Prophet Muhammed (pbuh) also shows that he himself made special arrangements for the education and training of women.

It is acknowledged from the Holy Quran and Hadiths that the acquisition of knowledge for women is the same for men.

From the above Hadiths, one infers that education is not only a right but also a responsibility of every Muslim, be it a male or female. Emphasis is also laid on the quality of education imparted to girls and women. Hadiths speak about the superiority of the person who seeks knowledge over the one who does not. The references here of superiority are to the person who seeks knowledge, irrespective of gender.

A survey reveals that most of the important compilers of Hadiths (sayings of Prophet Mohammed pbuh) from the earlier period, received many of them from women teachers, as the immediate authorities.

~~~~~~~~~~~~~~
~~~~~~~~~~~~~~

GREAT WOMEN IN ISLAMIC HISTORY

My keen study unfolded a list of women scholars of Islam who are also considered as the leading authorities on the teachings of Islam by reliable sources.

Indeed, throughout history, Muslim women contributed to the legacy of Islam as great martyrs, scholars, jurists, rulers, warriors, businesswomen, doctors, nurses and legal experts.

The vital experiences of Muslim women of the Middle East, South Asia, Africa and Europe from the Historic period of 7th to 21st century has been reiterated. A brief review of the lives, struggles and achievements of these great women is carried out within the existing socio-historical, cultural and religious practices across the globe.

One must be aware of the accomplishments of contemporary Muslim women (be it heads of state, scholars or activists). The fact that women also played a central role in the pre-Modern Muslim world as intellectuals, advisers, poets, mystics, rulers and warriors tend to stay undermined.

The time span between 8th to 14th century is largely marked as the Golden period of Islam - a historic period when, through battles, invasions, victory, defeat, trade, deals, and scholarly teachings, Islam spread and established itself from Morocco to Indonesia to Spain. Scholars from historical and religious disciplines testify that women occupied a much higher status,right at the advent of Islam than the years following the spread of Islam around the globe.

By sharing a handful of biographies of a few of these luminaries from Islamic history, it is my assumption that this will help eliminate certain beliefs (among both Muslims and non- Muslims) about the role of women in Islamic societies and trigger further concern and inquiry into women's history in the medieval and early modern Islamic world (as well as in pre-modern history generally).

A profound and thorough study of the lives of Khadija (RA), Umm Salama (RA) Aisha (RA), Hafsa (RA) and many others during the life and right after the death of Prophet Muhammad (Pbuh) affirm that these extraordinary women retained respect and power in society. They are respected as leaders, preachers, guides, scholars and most importantly the "Mother of Ummah."

1. Khadijah bint al – Khywaylid [RA]

Khadijahbint al-Khuwaylid is one of history's most notable women. The first wife of Prophet Muhammad (Pbuh) was not only a wealthy, successful and an esteemed tradeswoman but also the richest woman in Mecca at that time. Even before her marriage to Prophet Mohammed (pbuh), she was an important figure in her own right, as a successful merchant and one of the noblest figures of Mecca. She played an essential role in supporting Islam and has a distinction of being the first Muslim. Prophet Mohammed (pbuh) himself is believed to have said in a hadith preserved in Sahih Muslim, "God Almighty never granted me anyone better in this life than her. She accepted me when people rejected me; she believed in me when people doubted me; she shared her wealth with me, when people deprived me; and Allah granted me children only through her."

Khadija as a wife was a great supporter at every stage of our Prophet Mohammed (pbuh). When Mohammed (pbuh) first heard Angel Gabriel speaking to him, he was frightened. He then shared his encounter with the angel to Khadija. It was she who had comforted and convinced Muhammad to accept that Allah had spoken to him through Gabriel.

Khadija(RA)was also the first person to accept Islam, and she is mentioned as the "Mother of Believers." She assisted Muhammad during his time as a prophet both morally and financially.

2. Umm Salamah [RA]

Umm Salamah, also known as Hind bint Abi Umayya, was one of the most influential wives of Prophet Mohammad [pbuh]. She was born in Mecca in 580 or 596 AD and died in Madiah at the age of 86. She is recognized for recalling numerous Hadiths and life of Prophet Muhammaed [pbuh].

Umm Salamah had the honour of being one of the earliest converts to Islam.Prophet Muhammad [pbuh] is said to have chosen Umm Salama as a guardian of Al Syeda Fatima Al-Zahra [most prominent daughter of Muhammad (pbuh)] after Khadija died. Attributes that distinguished Umm Salamah included her role in the upbringing of Fatima Al-Zahra. Umm Salama proclaimed to have displayed true knowledge in all affairs and held a prominent role in the house of Muhammad [pbuh] and the society. She was known for her intelligence, political savviness, and activities in fighting for women's rights. Umm Salama possessed excellent judgmental qualities, rapid powers of reasoning and unparalleled abilities to formulate correct opinions. She often acted as Muhammad's Advisor during negotiations concerning the Treaty of Hudaybiyyah with Meccans in 628 AD. She was with Prophet Muhammed [pbuh] during the Battle of Banu Mustaliq, Taif, Khaybar, Hunayn and the conquest of Makkah.

Umm Salamah was wise, skillful and very learned in religious matters. She was very devoted to destitute and needy as well. Her life portrays her amiability and kindness towards all neighbours.

After the death of Prophet Muhammad [pbuh], Umm Salamah(RA) continued to have an influence on Islam. Nearly three hundred and eighty-seven Hadiths [sayings of Muhammad (pbuh)] were said to be received from Umm Salamah. Many used to consult her for points of Sharia (Islamic Laws) too. Her numerous transmissions of Hadiths, along with her strong character and contributions have had a lasting impact on Islam.

3. Aishah binte Abu Bakar [RA]

Aishah binte Abu Bakar, the youngest wife of Prophet Mohammed (pbuh) was extremely proficient and talented and possessed an extraordinary memory. As a Muslim Scholar, she is credited with narrating more than two thousand Hadiths and was esteemed for teaching renowned scholars. Some of Aishah's hadith review matters are related to Mohammad's [pbuh] personal life as a husband, father, friend, neighbour etc, which Muslims are meant to imitate, and a large number also analyses matters related with inheritance, pilgrimage, prayers, cleanliness, respect, relations, parents, offsprings, truth, evils and more. Aishah is known as a genius who was well informed about different subjects. She had a great affinity for learning and became noted for her intellect and sharp sense of judgment. Aishah worked to spread Islam and continued to do so after Mohammed's [pbuh] death. She is known to have established and taught at multiple schools before her death in 678 A.D.

Aishah played a political and military role in addition to passing along spiritual wisdom after Mohammed's (pbuh) death. A clear analysis of her life confirms that a woman can be a scholar, preacher,transmitter of knowledge, guide, leader, adviser, exert influence over men and women and provide them with inspiration and leadership. The example of Aisha (RA) promoting education, particularly the education of women in the laws and teachings of Islam is authentication for women education. She was a leader in every field of knowledge, society and politics.

4. Hafsa bint Umar [RA]

Hafsa bint Umar is also one of Prophet Muhammad's wives (pbuh). She was known for her memorization and preservation of the Quran after Prophet Muhammed's (pbuh) death.

Hafsa was born in the family of a great warrior and wrestler, Umar Bin Khattab (may Allah be pleased with him) who was well-known for his military skills. Umar ibn al-Khattab was the second caliph after the Prophet's (pbuh) death.

Hafsa was known for being powerful, obstinate, and educated. The Prophet (pbuh) admired Hafsa's ability to read and write which were exceptional among women at that time. She was skilful writer, orator and a keen follower of Islam. When Hafsa migrated from Mecca to Medina, she made special arrangements to memorize each verse. She would think deeply about them, paying special attention to its meaning, implications, and interpretations. Hafsa's enthusiasm for knowledge went above and beyond what was needed. She worked endlessly to gain knowledge and to transmit that knowledge for future generations. After the death of the Prophet Muhammad (pbuh), Hafsa(RA) was made liable for preserving and protecting the folios of the Quran which was finally assembled into a single document.

5. Fatima bint Muhammad [RA]

The youngest daughter of Prophet Muhammad [pbuh] from the first wife Khadija [RA] was born around 606-615 AD [dates mentioned for the birth, marriage and death of Fatima vary in different sources] in Mecca, Saudi Arabia. Fatima was bestowed with many titles, some of which include 'Al-Zahra' meaning 'the shining one', 'Al-Batul' and 'Al-Tahera' which refers to her pious nature that was of 'chaste, virtues and pure one'. Fatima Al-Zahra was embodied with the qualities of courage, loyalty, humility and selflessness. Fatima was very dear and loving to her father Prophet Muhammad [pbuh] which is mentioned in many Hadiths:

"Fatima is a part of my flesh; whoever causes her to be upset, upsets me." — Prophet Muhammad(pbuh) [Sahih Al- Bukhari]

Fatima holds a unique position as one of the most pious women ever. In addition to being a daughter of Prophet Muhammad [pbuh], she was the wife of Ali [RA] and mother of Hasan [RA], Hussain [RA], Umm Kulsum [RA] and Zainab [RA]. Amongst her most profound merits includes the one being referred by her father Muhammad [pbuh] as the "Greatest of women of the Heaven and the Earth."

Fatima [RA] had a compassionate and gentle personality. She was known to be deeply spiritual. She spent a simple and humble life by doing every work at home by herself, taking care of her family and helping the poor and needy in every possible way. Fatima was very active in the community too. She played a key role in the battles of Uhud and Trench by tending to the wounded and preparing food. She also supported her father in difficulties.

Fatima Al-Zahra had experienced and witnessed several instances of sadness and hardships in her life. She suffered the greatest tribulations at a very young age with the death of her mother Khadija [RA].

Death of her father Prophet Muhammad [pbuh] later left her in grief. Even after the death of her father [pbuh], Fatima displayed a significant amount of bravery, valor and courage. According to many historical sources, Syeda Fatima died less than six months after her father's death at the age of 24 or 28.

Fatima Al Zahra(RA) is one of the most revered women in the history of Islam. She remains a devout servant to the cause of Islam, sacrificing her comfort and luxuries with tranquility, and a true role model for every Muslim, especially women who follow her teachings and etiquettes.

6. Sumayyah bint Khayyat [RA]

The first martyr in Islamic history

Sumayyah bint Khabbat was an African woman who was born in 550 AD Mecca, Saudi Arabia. She was a freed slave. Sumayya played an important role in the history of Islam but was given the worst punishment for accepting Islam. She and her family members were tortured physically and mentally. Yet, despite the physical and mental pain, she remained stubborn and never refused to put all her faith in one god that is Allah. Although her husband was martyred before her eyes, Quresh pagans failed to convert Sumayyah. After a long period of torture, Abu Jahl stabbed her with his thirsty spear, causing her to attain Martyrdom. Sumayyah was killed, offering her sacrifice for Allah. She gained a unique position by becoming the first martyr in Islamic history. Thus, the fact remains that the first martyr in Islamic history is indeed a woman.

She was the seventh person to embrace Islam and one of the foremost companions of Prophet Muhammad (pbuh). Sumayyah along with her husband Yasir ibn Amir (RA) and son Ammar were amongst the earliest converts to Islam.

Summayah bint Khayyat (RA) is remembered for her strength, courage, and faith in a period when Muslims were heavily persecuted. Her active commitment to her faith shatters the image of Muslim women as oppressed beings who have no choice in regard to how they practice their faith.

7. Nusaybah Bint Ka'ab [RA]

The first woman Warrior of Islam

Nusaybah Bint Ka'ab, also named as Umm Ammarah was one of the first women to convert to Islam and a companion of Muhammad (pbuh). She was a warrior of the 7th century. She fought in numerous battles; from the battle of Uhud to the war of Yamama, she was famous for her strength and courageous participation in battle fields. Her skills were praised by the Prophet Muhammad (pbuh) himself.

From Ansar, she was one of the first two women of Madinah to pledge allegiance to the Prophet Muhammad (pbuh) despite knowing that if caught, she could be tortured or even killed by the Makkans.

During the battle of Uhud, the Muslims were on the verge of defeat, so Umm Ammarah, along with her husband and two sons, surrounded the Prophet (pbuh) to protect him from enemies. This proved that her courage was not restricted to the battlefield only. After watching both of her sons martyred, she displayed immense patience and strength. She further devoted herself to the education and training of the women in Madinah. She was a true inspiration and continues to remain even today.

Umm Ammarah(RA) and many other women also took part in different wars. Prophet Muhammad (pbuh) made them a part of the booty during the wars. She was also active during the treaty of Hudaibiyah. These exemplify the equality displayed by the Prophet (pbuh) to women in different situations.

8. Umm Al-Darda Al-Soghra (RA)

Umm al-Darda was a companion of Prophet Muhammad (pbuh).

She was a prominent jurist in Damascus in the 7th century. She was the wife of a famous sahaba Abu Darda and had learned the sciences of Hadiths. Imam Bukhari referred to her as an authority in Sahih al Bukhari: "UmmDarda.... she was an expert theologian."

She was an excellent scholar among women, and at the same time extremely religious and pious. Umm Darda became a teacher of hadith and fiqh. She taught in both Damascus, in the great Umayyad Mosque, and Jerusalem. Her classes were attended by Imams, Jurists, and Hadith scholars. Umm al-Darda had shown piety, modesty and unpretentiousness both in her daily life and teachings. She charged no fee for delivering knowledge and lived on charitable gifts.

According to the Saudi Gazette, Umm Al-Darda became a reliable authority for Hadith and taught several prominent Islamic figures and scholars, including Umayyad Caliph Abdul Malik Bin Marwan, as well as the celebrated scholar, theologian and Judge Hassan Al-Basri.

She viewed the exchange of knowledge as a form of worship and said:

"I have sought worship in everything, I did not find anything more relieving to me than sitting with scholars and exchanging knowledge with them."

9. Rufaida Al- Aslamia (RA)

The first female nurse and surgeon in Islam.

Rufaida Alaslam was born around 620 AD in Madina Al munawwara, Kingdom of Saudi Arabia. Under the guidance of her father Saad Alsalmy, a physician and a mentor, Rufaida obtained clinical experience. She is recognized as one of the the earliest converts to Islam. She was among women from Ansar who welcomed Prophet Muhammad (pbuh) on his arrival to Madina.

Rufaida was kind, patient, devoted, committed and an empathetic nurse. She practiced at the time of Prophet Muhammad(pbuh). She was also a social worker, who helped poor, orphan, handicapped people in need. She solved social problems associated with different diseases by promoting the importance of hygiene in the society and provided the people with health education.

With the permission from Prophet Muhammad (pbuh) she trained many Muslim girls and women as nurses. World's first code of nursing conduct and ethics was drafted by Rufaida bint Saad Aslamya.

Rufaida practiced her skills during many battles in her tents by providing first aid to injured soldiers, arranged shelter for the wounded, taking care of sick and dying, and made arrangements for drinking water in deserts. She participated in the battles of Badr, Uhad, Khandaq,Khaibar and others.

Several scholarly articles were written about her work. One of the great scholars Saud Hussain said,

"Rufaida devoted her life to the development and improvement of nursing. She succeeded in laying new rules and traditions as the basis of better nursing."

In Pakistan, the famous college of nursing and midwifery, The Aga Khan University was named after her. An annual Rufaida Al-Aslamia prize in Nursing is awarded at the University of Bahrain. Every year, the Royal College of Surgeons in Ireland(RCSI) at the University of Bahrain awards one student the prestigious Rufaida Al- Aslamia Award in Nursing.

Rufaida(RA) is a role model for every woman for her exceptional and outstanding participation and contribution in Islamic world.

10. Zainab bint Ali (RA)

She was the granddaughter of Prophet Mohammad (pbuh) from his daughter Fatima and her husband Ali ibn Abi Talib. She was born in Madinah in 626 AD. Zainab was six years old when her mother Fatima passed away. She took charge of her two elder brothers Hasan and Hussain. Soon, she became famous for her knowledge of the Holy Quran and her virtuous life. Zainab shared her knowledge with others and taught the women of Madina, precepts of Islam according to the Holy Quran and Hadiths.

In the Battle of Karbala 680 AD, Zainab was a prominent figure of Ahl al-Bayt (family of Prophet Mohammad pbuh). She played a key role both during and after the Massacre at Karbala (680), where her brother al-Hussain ibn Ali, and 72 of her nephews and other brothers were killed by Yazid. She was an effective leader of the Ahl al-Bayt and served as the primary defender of her brother, Hussain. At Kufa, she guarded her nephew Ali ibn al-Hussain (d.712) from certain death by the governor of the city and, being presented to the Yazid ibn Mu'awiya at Damascus.

In her lifetime, Zainab suffered massive pain from witnessing her loved ones martyred before her eyes, but she never objected to the fate decreed upon her by Allah. The agony she expressed was an outpouring of her incredible humanity. Zainab's role was ideal. Her role becomes even more impressive when one considers the period, which was patriarchal and male- dominant, and when women were suppressed. At that time, for a woman to stand, fight and speak the truth was not an easy task. It shows how bold and brave Muslim women were and how they played a prominent role in consolidating Islamic teachings. Her strength, patience and wisdom made her one of the most important women in Islam. Zainab(RA) is a great figure of sacrifice, courage, forbearance and devotion to Islam. She will continue to inspire the posterity.

11. Nafisa Bint Al-Hassan (RA) [9th Century]

The great-great-granddaughter of Prophet Muhammad (pbuh) was born in Mecca in 145 AH. She was a famous scholar of the 9th century in Egypt, Cairo, where a mosque now carries her name.

Nafisa Bint Al-Hassan was raised with extensive Islamic education. She memorized the entire Holy Quran and learned Hadiths at a very young age. She also studied Islamic jurisprudence in detail from great scholars. She extended her knowledge by providing religious instructions to women and girls. She taught two of the most outstanding scholars of all time - Al-Shafi'i and Ahmad ibn Hanbal. These teachings eventually lead to the Shafai and Hanbali schools of Islam respectively.

She was actively involved in the politics of society. In order to get rights met, people at the time of disputes with the ruler of Egypt would go to her to resolve their issues. She is a great inspiring role model for today's women.

Ibn Kathir made the following statement:

"She was a wealthy lady, did a lot of favors to the people, especially those paralysed, those with severe illness, and to all other ill people. She was a devout, ascetic, and of abundant virtue."

12. Shuhdah al-Baghdadiyyah [11th Century]

Shuhdah al-Baghdadiyah was known as Fakhr an-Nisa (Pride of womankind), "the writer of Baghdad" and al-Katibah, or the female scriber. Al-Baghdadiyyah was born in Iran and died in Iraq. She was a scholar, Muhaddith and a calligrapher. Shuhdha was called "the calligrapher, the pride of womanhood, al muhaddithat of Iraq."

Fakhr-un-Nisa Shuhdah was born in the early 11th century in the Iranian city of Dinawar to Abu Nasr Ahmed. Having studied under the guidance of her father, the famous traditionalist Abu Nasr al-Dinawari, as well as several reputed scholars, Al-Baghdadiyyah was known for accurately transmitting and explaining hadith [sayings of Prophet Mohammed pbuh].

She gave lectures at universities and mosques in Baghdad and her teachings of the hadith were held in high regard.

Apart from her extensive knowledge of the Prophet's sayings, she was known for her impeccable skills in calligraphy.

Her style of writing gained much popularity and was taken up generation after generation.

13. Fatima Al- Fudayliyya [18th Century]

Fatima was also known as Al-Shaykha Al-Fudayliyya bint Hamad al- Fudayliyya. She was an 18th- 19th century Muslim scholar of Hadith and jurist She had mastered the art of calligraphy and excelled in different Islamic sciences, with a special interest in Hadith.

Having studied from reputed scholars, she became a reliable source on Hadith, with students attending her lectures and receiving certificates from her. She was also highly regarded for her skills in writing books with beautiful calligraphy.

Among her most prominent students were Shaikh Omar Al-Hanafi and Shaikh Muhammad Salih.

Towards the end of her life, Al-Fudayliyya settled in Mecca where she founded a public library. She died in 1831(Hijri 1247).

14. Queen Zubaida

(Baghdad, Wife of Caliph Haroon Rashid)

Zubaida Khatoon was born in 148 A.H (766CE). Her real name is Amatul Aziz. She was very brilliant, pretty, wealthy and fond of learning. She learned the Holy Quran, Hadiths and Arabic Literature. She also showed great passion for Literature and Science and assigned funds inviting poets, scientists and literary figures to Baghdad.

It is said that her palace had a hundred women who were hafizaat of [memorized] Quran and who recited the Holy Quran day and night.

Wherever and whenever she went inside the palace, verses of the Holy Quran were heard.

She helped a group of Ulema to promote Islamic learning. She lived during the times of Imam al Shafai. She was married to Haroon Rashid in 165 AH. Queen Zubaida was a very loyal and committed Muslim. She performed the holy pilgrimage Hajj many times on foot with her husband, often making the 900-mile trip from Baghdad to Makkah.

Her greatest accomplishments were the planning and construction of a road project from Baghdad to Makkah. Deep wells, water pools, guest houses, mosques and police posts were made available to provide comfort and security to the pilgrims.

Zubaida's achievement was a canal named Ain Zubaida, to serve free water to pilgrims in all areas of Makkah. After several years of hard work, the canal was ultimately brought all the way from Hunain Valley to Jabal–e Rahma in Arafat, and then to Mina and Muzdalfa. The remains of this historical canal can still be seen on the side of Mount Arafat. Queen Zubaida is a figure of inspiration for every Muslim woman.

The above studies proclaim that Islam endorses women education and approves their active participation in every field of life by following Islamic rules and regulations. Had it not been so, the world would not have witnessed the shift of a society plunged in the darkness of hostility and predominance into one that was enlightened with philosophers, intellectuals, critics and scholars.

For leaders in some Islamic sects, practices that were considered inappropriate differed overtime like inheritance laws, marriage customs, family lineage and veiling practices. In addition, groups within Islam such as Shiites, Sufis, Kharijs and many more developed their own interpretations that differed from each other and from the mainstream of true Islamic interpretations. As a result, the lives of Muslim women from this vast and diverse region of civilization, cultures, languages and religions differed from one location to another. By studying the narratives of Muslim women across the globe, one will know the history of Islam through lives of women who lived as merchants, religious and political leaders, battle field warriors, scientists, inventors, advisors, poets, writers, queens, storytellers, slaves etc…

Indeed, throughout history, many Muslim scholars were involved in the founding of educational institutions. Most notable of this is Fatima al-Fihri, who established the university of Al-Qarawiyyin in 859 CE. The university remains, according to UNESCO and others, the oldest continually running university in the world.

Women have been making their mark on societies, changing the course of history at times and influencing different spheres of life. Muslim civilization is a shred of evidence that incredible women from different cultures, traditions and history worked alongside men to progress their communities. These inspiring stories, charismatic personalities and determination to contribute to the development of societies make them beacons of light that guide young women to the path of progress today.

Women competed in all the fields of life. There were women who surpassed educational and cultural efforts like Fatima Al-Fihri, and others who transcended in mathematics such as Sutayta al-Mahamil. Many outshined in the medical field, administration and management, philosophy and arts. They played central roles and ruled important territories in the Muslim civilization, some of those which included Labana of Cordoba of 10th century (Spain), Sitt al-Mulk of 11th century (Egypt), Melike Mama Hatun of 12th century (Turkey), Razia Sultana of Delhi of 13thcentury (India) and others.

I pay gratitude to these outstanding women and highlight their participation, believing that this research into an unchanged script would focus light on women achievers from all over the world.

It is a fortunate time to echo on the reality that historical women from around the world and from all walks of life, had either been leaders or been fundamental to fight for domestic rights, community rights, governmental rights, national rights, environmental justice and equality.

The Modern Environmental Movement is inspired by the bold writings about human impact on nature by an American Biologist, Ecologist, Writer and Scientist Rachel Carson more than fifty years ago. Her work includes "Silent Spring", "Under the Sea-Wind", "The Sea Around Us."

In the last decade, Rosa Louise McCauley Parks, [1913 – 2005] an American activist in the civil rights movement was identified as the "Mother of Freedom Movement" on account of her fearless rejection to give up her bus seat for the white passenger.

The Chipko Movement in India in the early 1970s concerning the tree-hugging women activated environmentalists all around the globe by ceasing the cutting of thousands of trees and making a human circle around them, even by endangering their own lives.

There are endless instances to go through. Though some of these women are named, a bulk majority of others remain hidden and nameless.

It is quite rare to hear examples of Muslim women leaders too. Even though many Muslim women have been the head of states in recent times, the modern world has delayed their due recognition and presence.

Recently, we lost Asma Jahangir, a valiant of human rights from Pakistan. She was a lawyer and an activist who established the first-ever all-women juridical firm in Pakistan and was one of the leading protectors of women rights and human rights. As a lawyer, Asma opposed the practice of bonded labourers in Pakistan and as a UN envoy, she guarded the rights of the Rohingya of Myanmar, the Kashmiris, the Palestinians, and the Christians in Pakistan.

Sadly, many such Muslim women have been forgotten, or perhaps not even remembered, in the very long history of Muslim women's eminence from time immemorial.

Hearing about muslim women is very rare and unusual!! Why is this so?

In reality, from the time immemorial, Muslim women's stories have been wiped off and assigned to mere footnotes and even the resources for the acknowledgement of such Muslim women these days is very little. The way Muslims and Islam followers are presented in the mainstream is abundant with a pattern - it involves the description of Muslim women, often conferred as static victims of male patriarchy who are simply ignorant of their own cruelty, abuse, injustice, dictatorship and domination and must be told often that they are oppressed, they are oppressed!!!!

I would like to build a space for all the Muslim women, as history has forgotten the Muslim women who deserve a place in our textbooks and the women whose voices should echo.

This research allowed me to uncover things I did not know. There are countless Muslim women who have given great contributions to the world. These women took responsibility for themselves and did things on their own. The history of Muslim women is a history of action, wisdom, intellect and tolerance. It is a history of potential, enthusiasm, and strength.

15. FATIMA AL-FIHIRI

(Morocco, Died in 880)

The world's first university (still in operation) was founded by a Muslim woman in the history of mankind!!!! As recognized by the Guinness Book of World Records and UNESCO, a very intellectual, smart and generous Muslim woman from Tunisia, Fatima bint Muhammad Al-Fihriya Al-Qurashiya was credited for founding the oldest existing, continually operating a first degree-awarding educational institution in the world - the University of Al Quaraoulyine in Fes, Morocco in 859 CE.

It was over 1,000 years ago in the 9th century that the concept of an institution for academic learning and research was born from the foundation of the very first brick laid by Fatima Al-Fihri, a wealthy widow who invested all her inheritance into financing the Al-Qarawiyyin Mosque which later became a University, world's First Grade granting institution of higher learning. Her idea of an educational hub that provided opportunities for advanced learning spread throughout the world in the Middle Ages, resulting in some of Europe's oldest institutions in the following centuries, including the University of Bologna (founded in 1088) and the University of Oxford (founded around 1096). Pope Sylves 2, who is recognized for having introduced zero and Arabic numerals to Europe, also learned that at Morrocan University. Keeping this in mind, one can view Fatima as a real leader who contributed to the Muslim world by flipping the stereotype of ignorant, uncivilized Muslims. She established the concept of a university as one knows it today.

The influence that was left behind after al-Fihri's death resulted in the expansion of the university. The mosque-turned-school soon became the largest one in Africa, with a capacity of over 22,000 students. Al-Qarawiyyin University is still going strong; notable alumni include Fatima al-Kabbaj, one of the first female students, who later became the sole female member of the Moroccan Supreme Council of Religious Knowledge.

16. Mariam al-Asturlabi [Syria, 10th Century]

Mariam was a Muslim scientist, mathematician and astronomer. Born in Syria in the 10th century, she was famous for developing Astrolabes i.e. navigational devices used to locate and predict the position of the sun, stars, etc., and to determine the latitudes using local time and vice versa.

Maryam al-Asturlabi is also described as "one of the many brilliant women of her time." Mariam learned the art from her father and excelled in it. Her genius level intellect made her designs superior to others and the Astrolabes designed by her were more intricate and innovative.

Astrolabes gained immense importance and popularity in the Muslim era because they could be used to understand the timings of sunrise, sunset and thus, the times of Salat.

Mariam had made a significant contribution to society. Her work and her quest to gain, use and share knowledge for the benefit of everyone has to be admired. She exemplified that the pursuit of knowledge has always been encouraged in Islam, and does not discourage women from it. She pursued studies and helped innovate new technology for her time. Mariam al- Astrolabiya remains a role model in the present times.

17. NANA ASMA'U [Nigeria, 1793-1864]

Nana Asma'u, Daughter of Usman 'dan Fodio, a nineteenth-century Muslim scholar, was born in 1793 in the region now known as northern Nigeria. She was a poet, and educator of both men and women. She was educated in the Quran as well as Arabic,

Fulfulde, Hausa, and Tamacheq Tuareg. She was also an activist who used her poetic work to promote Islam. She proudly sits in the pantheon of the great educators of Africa.

Probably the most impressive thing about her life was how she got a group of female teachers together and travelled across Nigeria, including the rural villages with the goal of educating other women. Ultimately, Nana Asma'u was someone who dedicated her life to uplift the minds of her counterparts.

The present written works by Asma'u are relevant to Islamic Education. She was responsible for women's religious education for most of her life. She fought for women rights publicly and privately. She was surrounded by scholarly and educated women and grew to be a prolific writer, visionary and authoritative figure. Her legacy for generations of strong African women, who still refer to her example, demonstrates the real transformative effect she had on her society.

Her ingenious educational system is set as a wall of justice, pushing back against prejudice and uplifts women in every community. She lives a legacy for young men and women around the world; a legacy of social advancement, cultural progress and spiritual enlightenment. Her legacy for Muslims is especially poignant. As the community struggles to spark female voices in scholarships, her words echo forth and call us all to make space for our women scholars, to strengthen our women students of knowledge and to open institutions for female education and leadership. The legacy of Nana Asma'u leaves a mark on every woman who depicts a deep concern for her community and wishes to commit her life to scholarship and positive cultural change. Although Nana Asma'u died in 1864, her legacy is still strong in Northern Nigeria.

Many organizations, schools and meeting halls are named in her honour. She has been an example of the role of women in Islam in the 21st century.

18. Bedour Al-Maghrabi, Maha Al-Qahtani and Thekra Al-Otaibi

(Saudi Arabia, Students of Princess Nourah University - Present)

Saudi female students from Princess Nourah bint Abdul- Rahman University were awarded the first place during the 2015 British Invention Show for inventing a device that can be used for sense rehabilitation and stimulation in patients with sensory neuropathy issues. According to Arab News, the basic premise of the device is based on the innovation of a new multi-sensory stimulation program, which impaired sensory systems and improves the affected cell's function. The same invention was ranked as second place at Korea's International Women's Invention Exposition in 2014.

Furthermore, Al-Maghrabi and Al-Qahtani invented glasses for people with cerebral blindness which could help them identify anything in their surroundings. The glasses can draw a picture of the area around the patient and define it through spoken words after analyzing it through a mobile app and send it through an earpiece.

19. FATIMA BEEVI [India, born on 30th April 1927]

Fatima Beevi etched her name permanently into the history by becoming the first female judge of the Supreme Court. Fatima was born on 30th April 1927 at Pathanamthitta, Travancore now, in the state of Kerala, as the daughter of Annaveetil Meera Saheb and Khadeja Bibi.

She did her schooling from Catholicate High School, Pathamthetta, her BSc from University College, Thiruvananthapuram and obtained her degree from Govt Law College, Thiruvananthapuram.

Fatima Beevi was appointed as the Judge of the Supreme Court of India in 1989. With the appointment to the tribunal, she became the first female judge of the Supreme Court and the First Muslim woman to be appointed to any higher judiciaries in the Country. On her retirement from the court, she served as a member of the National Human Rights Commission and later as the Governor of the Indian States of Tamil Nadu from 1997 to 2001. She also served as Chancellor of Madras University.

She received a D.Litt and Mahila Shiromani Award in 1990. She was also presented with the Bharat Jyoti Award.

The story of Fatima Beevi, a woman who dared to go beyond the obvious boundaries and went on to become India's First Supreme Court Judge remains unforgettable. The Supreme Court Collegium of India created history when it picked Fatima Beevi as the first woman advocate to be recommended for the appointment as a Judge of the Supreme Court, which has had just six women Judges in 68 years.

Justice Fatima Beevi broke all the barriers of societal biases to take up a profession that was once considered to be a Man's prerogative.

In October 1989, six months after retiring from Kerala High Court, Fatima was appointed as a Supreme Court Judge. For India, it was a watershed moment that paved the way for women in India to occupy a position in Higher Judiciary.

There have been only eight female judges of the supreme court of India till today. Fatima Beevi continues to be a role model for every woman aspiring to enter the historically male-dominated space of the courtroom which was like a forbidden fruit for women.

20. SHIRIN EBADI [Born on 21st June 1947 — Present]

Ebadi, the first Muslim woman to win the Nobel Peace Prize was born in Iran in 1947. She is an Iranian lawyer, political activist, writer, teacher, former Judge, human rights activist and founder of Defenders of Human Rights centre in Iran.

Shirin Ebadi received her graduation degree from the law department at the University of Tehran in 1965. Soon after graduation, she passed the qualifying exam to become a Judge in 1969. She received a Doctorate's degree in Law in 1971. In 1975, she became the first woman president of the Tehran City Court and served until 1979. Ebadi became the first woman Judge in Iran when she was just 23 years old. By 2004, Ebadi worked as a Lecturer at Law College in the University of Tehran. She is a campaigner for strengthening the legal status of children and women and has also defended various child abuse cases.

Ebadi was awarded the Nobel Peace Prize on October 10th 2003 for her efforts in establishing democracy and human rights, especially for the rights of women and children and political prisoners in Iran. Since then, Ebadi has lectured, taught and received several awards in different countries, issued statements and defended people accused of political crimes in Iran. She has travelled and spoken to the audience in India, the United States, and other countries. She also released her autobiography. With other five Nobel Laureates, she created the

Nobel Women's initiative to promote peace, justice and equality for women.

In addition to being an internationally recognized advocate of human rights, she has also established many non-governmental organizations in Iran, including a campaign demanding an end to legal discrimination against women in Iranian law. Dr. Ebadi is also a university professor. She has published over 70 articles and 13 books dedicated to various aspects of human rights, some of which were published by UNICEF. In 2004, she was named by Forbes Magazine as one of the '100 Most Powerful Women' in the world.

Ebadi is crowned to be the first Muslim woman to receive a Nobel Peace Prize and only the fifth Muslim to receive a Nobel Prize in any field. She is a true inspiration for every woman. She is strong, brave and proud for not just Iran and Iranians, but also for the whole world and women specifically.

21. TAWAKKOL KARMAN [Born on Feb 1979 — Present]

Tawakkol Karman was born on 7th February 1979 in Yemen. She earned an undergraduate degree in Commerce from the University of Science and Technology, a graduate degree in Political Science from the University of Sanaa and an Honorary Doctorate in International Law from the University of Alberta in Canada.

Karman is a Yemeni journalist, politician, human rights activist, and a mother of three kids. She founded the WJWCC (Women Journalists Without Chains) to provide journalists with a platform to advocate for their freedom by reporting human rights abuses in her own country of Yemen. At the age of 32, she was the youngest Nobel Peace Prize Laureate (but was later replaced by Malala).

Tawakkal is known as "Mother of the Revolution" and was awarded the Nobel Peace Prize in 2011 in recognition of her work in the nonviolent struggle for the safety of women and for women's rights to full participation in peacebuilding work in Yemen. Upon being awarded the prize, Tawakkal became the first Yemeni, the first Arab woman, and the second Muslim woman to win a Nobel Peace Prize, as well as the Youngest Nobel Peace Laureate at the age of 32.

By shaping her society on her own terms, Karman flips the idea of the "white saviour narrative" on one's head. Like many others in Yemen, she is a proactive, outspoken figure, who rises to the occasion herself. She does not need to be saved.

22. MALALA YOUSUFZAI [12th July 1997 - Present]

Malala Yousufzai was born on 12th July in an educated Pashtun family in the Swat District of Northwestern Pakistan. Malala, an activist for female education is the youngest woman to be awarded the Nobel Prize. Taliban [an extremist and terrorist group] had begun to control the valley with its growing influence and leading socio-political power in that region. As a young girl, Malala had a great passion to gain knowledge. Eventually, the situations in the valley changed.

Girls were stopped from going to school. Cultural activities like dancing and watching television were prohibited. Females were not allowed to participate in any of the social activities. The Taliban oppose education for girls and it was an essential element of a terror campaign. The campaign spread its terrorism through destruction of nearly 400 schools by the end of 2008. It was Malala who challenged the Taliban in Pakistan and demanded girls' education. Malala blogged her experiences about the Taliban's rule for the BBC since 2009 and expressed her disagreement for the forcible establishment of false regulations in 2012.

In response to Malala's confrontation, one day, the Taliban attempted to assassinate Malala Yousafzai on the bus home from school. She suffered severe injuries, but survived and underwent several operations in the UK, where she lives today. In addition to her own education, she continues to work for the rights of girls to education.

During a speech at the United Nations on her 16th birthday in 2013, Malala shifted her focus on education and women's rights. She urged world leaders to change their politics. She also demanded action against illiteracy, poverty and terrorism. She quoted, "The extremists were, and they are afraid of books and pens. The power of education frightens them. They are afraid of Women...........

Let us pick up our books and pens. They are our powerful weapons." Malala Yousufzai.

Malala at the age of 17, in October 2014, created history by getting honoured as the youngest Nobel Peace Prize winner along with Kailash Satyarthi from India. In addition to the Nobel Peace Prize, she received many awards and honours nationally and internationally. She stands as a symbol of pride for her nation. Malala remains a zealous supporter of female education. She became a global motivator and teacher by a simple and firm act of going to school and a passion for learning. Her efforts and accomplishments are exceptional.

~~~~~~~~~~~~~~
~~~~~~~~~~~~~~

WOMEN EMPOWERMENT IN ISLAMIC SYSTEM OF LIFE

The wrong interpretations of Quranic verses and Hadiths, ignorance of Islamic teachings, biased propaganda of anti-Islamic ideology and prejudiced media has resulted in a wrong image of women in Islam; especially, that they are deprived of freedom and equality, when in fact, it's just the opposite.

Contrary to popular belief, Islam has uplifted the position of women. Heaven is laid at the feet of mothers. Fathers with two or three daughters, who take good care of them, give them education, treat them with kindness and equality and get them married to good men are rewarded with paradise. Brothers who are kind and good to their sisters are rewarded abundantly.

Thus, Islam teaches and encourages men to be good to their women. When one looks back in history before the advent of Islam, women were considered to be the source of all evil in Greek Mythology.

In the name of art, the Greeks depicted women in such a way that promoted unbridled sex.

During the Roman civilization, Philosopher Seneca reprimanded Romans about the degenerating family system. A sport named Ploratia promoted the licentious atmosphere.

Aristotle declared: "The female state is a deformity."

A Roman Catholic Aquinas believed: "A female is a misbegotten male."

Nietzsche, the German Philosopher opines," Woman is the source of folly, unreason."

In Modern Europe, women were not given equal rights and the situation led to several feminist movements that are constantly struggling for equal rights for women till date.

Before the advent of Islam in Arabia, the position of the fair sex was appalling. Girls were sometimes killed as soon as they were born. Infant girls were buried alive. A man could marry an abandon or divorcee any number of times. The number of wives was unlimited. Islam emancipated women in all respects.

1. **Freedom** - Thus, in pre Islamic period back to history, women were very miserable part of humankind. Women were suppressed, inherited, shackled, tortured, tyrannized and treated as sex object. Women were the properties of society, one could be exploited by all the men in the society, just like water, fire, land etc.[reference Islamic history books like Al Fiqh as sirah by Dr. Al Buthy, Raikul Makhtum by Al Mubarakfuri] 'Inheriting' of women was the common tradition. Almighty Allah says, "O thou who believe! Thou are forbidden to inherit women against their will." [Quran-4:19]

   In order to give women their rights, save them from discrimination, lowness, persecution, adversity, rejection, ruction, oppression and erase their misery, Allah honored women with high position by dedicating a whole chapter with numerous verses in favor of women in Holy Quran named ' An Nisa', means Women. Islam positioned women on high and noble place.

Islam has elevated the position of women in the roles of daughters, sisters, wives and mothers. Getting education became the foremost importance for every mankind regardless of gender. Women were permitted to own properties, earn their living, run their own business. Women got freedom to marry men of their choice and divorce if circumstances become difficult. A widow or divorcee is allowed to remarry if she wishes. Birth of a daughter was considered worthless by society, Allah blessed Prophet Muhammad (pbuh) with four daughters. And the relationship of father and daughter is presented from the life of prophet Muhammad (pbuh). Women were not entitled to inherit anything. Islam came with verses in Quran that gives women their rights of inheritance. Quran gives women their freedom, rights and teaches true Islam, and explains the laws of inheritance, relationships, chastity, cleanliness and may more. Thus Women in Islam enjoys full freedom under the boundries of Shariya[Islamic Laws].

People who voice women in Islam are oppressed are mistaken. Islamic history, Quanic teachings, life of Prophet Muhammad(pbuh) and laws of Islam that is Shariya must be their reference.

2. **Equality** - Islam promotes equality.
   The concept of justice and equality is the foundation upon which the Islamic system of Law is built. " For verily, God sent His Messangers and revealed His Scriptures so that Humanity may establish justice."writes Ibn al- Qayyim, stating the Quranic verse 57:25 that messengers were sent "so that people may uphold justice."

   Allah addresses, "O people, we created you from the same male and female, and rendered you distinct peoples and tribes that may recognize one another. The best among you in the sight of God is the most righteous. God is Omniscient, Cognizant."[Quran-49:13]

The Noble Qur'an mentions that every human is the descendent of one man Adam therefore, bothers to one another. Throughout the Quranic text, significance is laid on equality and justice with all, that includes one's enemy regardless of gender or ethnicity.

Prophet Muhammad (pbuh) said: "None of you (truly) believes until he wishes for his brother what he wishes for himself."

In another verse of Quran Allah emphasizes on justice and equality, " O you who believe! Be maintainers of justice, bearers of witness of Allah of Allah's sake, though it may be against your own selves or (your) parents or near relatives; if he is rich or poor, Allah is nearer to them both in compassion; therefore do not follow (your) low desires, lest you deviate; and if distort or turn aside, then surely Allah is aware of what you do. [Quran-4:135]

Many Islamic Scholars declare that there is nothing in Quran that treats women unequally. Instead they proclaim, Muslim women have been marginalized by cultural practices and dominant patriarchal system. Equality throughout the Quran is emphasized repeatedly irrespective of gender, caste, religion, region or color.

Holy Qur'an States: "Serve God, and join not any partners with Him; and do good- To parents, orphans, those in need, neighbours who are near, neighbours who are strangers; the companions by your side, the traveller, and what your right hands possess: Indeed Allah does not like those who are self-deluding and boastful."[Qur'an- 4:36]

The above verse clearly reveals the actions of equality and justice with every individual may it be your parents or parents of others, strangers, neighbours far or near , orphans and those in need known or unknown irrespective of religion and gender.

"Men deny us equality, not the Qur'an." A female Islamic judge in India speaks out in the newspaper 'The Guardian'

3. **Security** - Islam gives security to women at every stage of life. Prophet Muhammed (pbuh) said, "The person to whom a daughter is born and he does not give out preferential treatment to boys, Allah will reward him with heaven." – (Hadith)

   The responsibility of providing food, shelter and security lies with the male guardian. Parents are motivated to treat their female children equal to males.

   Prophet Muhammed (pbuh) said, "You should feed her [wife] when you eat, and clothe her when you yourself put on clothes. And in case of temporary boycott due to strained relations, it should be limited to the four walls of your house." - (Hadith) When a woman travels a long distance, a male guardian must accompany her to facilitate the journey. Islam restricted the number of wives to four. Divorce, though permissible, is not encouraged.

4. **Economic Empowerment** - Islam declares pursuing education a religious duty, which simultaneously binds over men and women.[Ibn Majah 1952]. Islam also allows women to be engaged in different economic activities[Hasan 1994] Khadija Prophet Muhammed's (pbuh) first wife was an eminent businessperson. Infact Muhammad(pbuh) was her employ before marrying her. There are many examples in Islamic history which shows women companions of Prophet Muhammad(pbuh) participated in different activities.The second caliph, Umar ibn Al- Khattab, appointed a woman ,Ash-Shifaa'bint Abdullah, as a supervisor of markets in Madinah. Wife of Abdullah ibn Mas'ud met her expenses by manufacturing and selling handicrafts. A female companion of Prophet(pbuh) said," I am a woman who buys and sells things."then different questions relating to business were asked by her. Several Muslim women of that time such as Khula, Lakhmia, Thaqafia, and bint Mukhramah traded perfumes. Thus, business was a genuine activity of the women companions of Prophet Muhammad (pbuh), [Crescentlife, n.d].Abu- Shuqqah(1990) a renowned scholar states in his voluminous work , " Women's Liberation at the Time of the

Prophet," more than 300 authentic traditions of the Prophet that confirms women active participation and contribution in social activities during Prophet's (pbuh)time.

Muhammad (pbuh) is known to have given equal treatment to both men and women in matters relating to education and economic empowerment. Economic and social empowerment of women no doubt is not possible without education, are keys to better life for Muslim Women. Prophet(pbuh) encouraged women at many instances for their skills.

Now my question is; Why most of the Muslim men in the names of Mohd, Ahmed, Rahim, Ali, Sultan and many more, impose restrictions on women for education and empowerment, when the teachings of Islam do not deny them to get educated and empowered?

Lives of Prophet Muhammad's (pbuh) wives and companions are true examples of women's participation in every field. Women proved successful from homemaking to battlefield. Illiteracy of girls grow them to be unprepared mothers, where parenting skills lag, resulting them unequipped to deal with modern problems like drugs, advanced technologies, different crimes etc.

Patriarchal structure of society denies women of Economic empowerment. The sufferings of women in underpowered economic system cannot be overlooked. Women with incredible skills and abilities are restricted at home only with the fear of her empowerment. This is the reality of many Muslim families. According to a Muslim Journalist AL-Momin, "When you make women suffer, you make the whole family suffer. This is why women rights are important! It is not about women, it is about families."

A Sociologist from Arab World states, "Women because of restrictions and because of this unequal kind of opportunity that they are facing in this society, have become great fighters, and they have become great achievers."

5. **Dignity** - The amount of dignity and respect given to the women in Islam are uncomparable with any other religion. In contrast to the Christian ideology i.e. woman is the source of evil and she opened the door to Satan, Islam believes that Satan simultaneously seduced both Adam and Hawa. The mother's place is higher than the fathers. Heaven lies under the mother's feet. A woman is the ruler or queen of her husband's establishment. The veil is only a protective device to shield her from mischievous staring eyes. When women are asked to wear a veil, men are ordered not to stare at them.

   Dress code for women in Islam is to insure woman's dignity and integrity. Women are enjoined to cover their bodies and lower their gaze in the presence of men. Nonetheless, these rules of dress and behavior appears restrictive to western world, serve a social function. Protection of dignity is a basic requirement in Islamic teachings for both men and women.

   In Holy Qur'an Allah declares, "In God's eyes, the most honored of you are the ones most mindful of Him: God is all knowing, all aware." (Quran-49:13)

   Concept of modesty in Islam is holistic, and applies to both men and women. Allah created Men and Women with unique physiological and psychological attributes. These differences are the vital components of a healthy family and community structure. Both are encouraged to be modest, Women dress code is obviously different from that of men. As Women possess beauty and attraction, and to protect them from sexual predators, sexual violence and different crimes modest dress code is obligatory. Final goal is to please God and to maintain a stable dignified society.

   Almighty Allah says, "And tell the believing women to reduce (some) of their vision...." - *(Quran 24: 31)*

Thus, Islam promotes equality, freedom, dignity, security, economic empowerment, and freedom of thought and expression to women. Islam is a religion that aims to ascertain, uplift and sustain the honour and dignity of women. The most important gift that Islam can grant to women is the knowledge of herself, her rights, her surroundings, the knowledge of the universe, the life phenomenon, relations, and the best ways to lead a successful and prosperous life. Islam encourages women to gain knowledge which helps her to know her place as well as her role and her purpose of existence. Indeed, knowledge is the greatest blessing that a woman enjoys in Islam. It is a demonstration of a woman's honourable dignified position that she occupies in the hierarchy of Islamic beliefs, values and principles. It is due to this that the Quran often articulates such testimonials.

"Which of the favors of Lord will you deny?" (Quran-Surah Rahman)

~~~~~~~~~~~~~~
~~~~~~~~~~~~~~

INDIAN HISTORY

As an Indian, it is my Right and Duty to honour and pay tribute to all the Great Women of India whose contributions can never be forgotten. India is a democratic country, where one dwells, grows and flourishes with people of different religions, cultures, languages and traditions. One cannot ignore the educational philosophy of our great educationists and social reformers like Savitribai Phule, Mother Teresa, Pandita Ramabai, Tara Bai Shinde, Anandi Gopal Joshi, Arali Gupta, Bechendripal, Fatima Beevi, Indira Gandhi, Kalpana Chawla, Kiran Bedi, and many more. Indian women who have been withstanding difficulties in a traditional-bound society since ages have now proved that their place is not only at home and hearth. They also have the ability to showcase their hidden talents in other fields that are dominated by men. They have realised that the sky is their limit. As a result, many Indian women have now also begun working as a pilot in the commercial sector and Airforce, as CEOs and advisers in best and leading companies, businesses women, trainers and motivators.

In the last several decades, they have made a long leap, achieving success with such hard work and indomitable spirit that nobody could even guess their sustained upward mobility in whichever field they are working currently. They taught us how to overcome challenges, and gave us strength, courage and confidence. They showed us the power of positivity, trust, love and kindness. Education helps women fight all kinds of evil and lets them stay aware of their rights, perhaps the only way through which they can bring a revolutionary change in any field they like. We are lucky to have incredible examples of such successful and thriving women around us.

These great women have become our ideal role models through their inspiring tales of struggle, determination, dedication, passion and their abilities to overcome every hurdle in life, only to reach those heights where the world can see them flying with bright colours.

They have dedicated their entire lives to their passion and proved to the world that nothing is impossible for women.

Rewinding the past, India has displayed Indian women as pioneers who irrespective of gender barriers, discrimination, lack of resources and support from the family and society have worked hard for their rights and emerged victorious in the field of education, literature, politics, arts, science, law, medicines, sports, and many more.

From Jhansi Ki Rani to Irom Sharmila, Indian women have always stood up for their rights and fought their battles despite restrictions and limitations. They are the shining beacons of hope who display/ed exemplary dedication in their respective fields every single day.

From Sita in Ramayana to Jhansi's Rani Laxmi bai, these women have triggered major social changes. India is blessed to have such extraordinary great women.

From Mrs. Vijay Laxmi Pandit, the first Indian woman President of UN General Assembly and Sarojini Naidu to Indra Gandhi, the second woman PM in the world and Kalpana Chawla to Prathibha Patil, the first woman president of India, the impact of women in the society is truly invaluable. Their commitment to the society in whole and to women, in particular, is rather significant. A woman is an essence of love, affection, sacrifice, care and the ability to nurture life.

Let's talk about a few in detail.

1. Razia Sultana

The first and last female Muslim ruler of the Delhi Sultanate (1205- 1240).

Razia Sultana was South Asia's first female Muslim ruler and daughter of Shams-ud-din Iltutmish and Qutub Begum. She was born in Budaun, Uttar Pradesh in C. 1205. She ruled the court of Delhi from 1236 to 1240. She was a talented, brave, and wise administrator and a great warrior. She belonged to the Turkish Seljuks ancestry. She received training in fighting and leading armies and also learned to administer kingdoms. She overcame conflicts over her gender and her slave ancestry.

When Iltutmish passed away on 30th April 1236, Razia delegated his rightful heir and was handed with the reign to the kingdom. Razia Sultana set up a proper law and order system and made governmental reforms in her territory. She tried to improve the infrastructure of the country by encouraging trade, building roads, digging wells, and establishing schools and libraries. In the field of arts and culture, Razia showed great contribution by encouraging poets, painters and musicians. Thus, she worked hard to strengthen the kingdom. She displayed her abilities as an excellent administrator. A secular ruler, Razia actively contributed to safeguarding and promoting the inherent culture of the Hindu subjects in her reign. She established schools, and centres for research and academics apart from public libraries that had Quran, the traditions of the Prophet as well as works of ancient philosophers.

When Razia was in Bathinda, on a visit with her husband, her half-brother, Muiz ud-din Bahram declared himself the Sultan of the

Mamluk dynasty. Razia, in an attempt to regain her throne, assembled forces and marched towards Delhi. She was, however, defeated by Bahram and killed.

2. Rani Laxmi Bai

The leading female warrior of India's first struggle for Independence [19th November 1828 – 17th June 1858].

Rani Laxmi Bai, also known as Jhansi Ki Rani or the Queen of Jhansi was one of the leading warriors of the 1857 war of independence.

She was a symbol of bravery, patriotism, honour and embodiment of courage at the time of British reign in India. Rani Laxmi Bai was born on 19th November 1828 at Poona. Her actual name was Manikarnika. She had a bright spark of fierce independence even at a young age, and her studies included horsemanship, archery, and self-defence. In 1842, Rani Laxmi Bai got married to Raja Gangadhar Rao who was the Maharaja or King of Jhansi. After marriage, she came to be known as Laxmi Bai.

Her valiant battle to ensure that her adopted son was recognized as the legal ruler of Jhansi may not have ultimately resulted in victory, but she continues to remain a beacon for the upcoming generation of freedom fighters.

Rani Laxmi Bai was a brave woman who stood up to the Britishers when they wanted to seize her kingdom and declare ownership. In her fight for independence, Rani Laxmi Bai showed utmost fearlessness, which the British army feared along with her undying determination and military skills. During the 1858 battle against the British army, Rani Laxmi Bai lost her life, but the Britishers were not convinced until her body had been burnt. This speaks volumes of how ossified the Britishers were of the one Indian woman who challenged them with her patriotic zeal and sovereignty.

3. Fatima Shaik

The first Muslim woman teacher in the Indian society.

Fatima Shaikh, like many Muslim Indian activists and reformers, has remained forgotten or erased from the history of India. Very little literature is available on the life, work and achievements of Fatima, even though Phule's recognition of the world was not possible without the association of Fatima with Savitribai Phule in her struggle for girls' education.

As India's first Muslim teacher, Fatima Shaikh started a 'Beti Padhao' Movement in the 19th century. She worked with Phule to establish the first school for girls at her own house, along with her brother Usman Shaikh in 1948.

When the Phule couple decided to educate women and girls of the lower class, they were rejected and opposed by their own family members and were asked to leave their home. It must be remembered that during those days, education was meant only for the higher class.

Upon the refusal from their family, they were not allowed to enter their own house. In such circumstances, they were offered refuge by Fatima and Usman. They not only enlightened their ambition of spreading education to the lower caste girls and women but also sheltered them. At the Shaikh's house, Fatima supported and helped Savitribai to establish the first-ever school for girls in Pune. It was known as the 'Indigenous Library'.

Despite facing many challenges and opposition from both the Hindu and Muslim communities, Fatima approached every household in her neighbourhood and community and encouraged them for girl's education. Fatima Shaikh played an important and active role, irrespective of gender, religion, or caste, ensuring that children had equal access to education.

4. Savitribai Phule

The first woman teacher of India [3rd January 1831 – 10th March 1897].

Savitribai Phule was born on 3rd January 1831 at Naigaon in Maharashtra's Satara district. She was an Indian social reformer, educationist, author and poet from Maharashtra. She was 'the first female teacher of India'.

Savitri was not educated at the time of her marriage. She was from a backward class and the dominant class did not allow backward communities and women to receive an education.

Savitri at the age of 17 along with her husband Jyotiba who was 21, opened a school for women in 1848. It was the country's first-ever school for women, started by Indians.

Phule was taught by her husband Jyotiba at their home. Later, she received a teacher's training course at an institute run by an American Missionary.

The couple was criticized by both families and communities for this step. They were threatened, harassed and humiliated socially. Cow dung, stones and mud were thrown at Phule when she walked to the school.

Savitribai's friend Fatima Shaikh served as a big support system to the Phule couple for starting a school for girls.

Phule was a fiery author/writer and poetess. Her writings include 'Kavya Phule' in 1854 and 'Bavankashi Subodh Ratnakar' in 1892. Her poem 'Go Get Education' urges the oppressed communities to get an education and break free from the chains of oppression. Phule died on 10th March 1897, while caring for a patient in a clinic who was affected by the bubonic plague.

Her achievements were diverse and numerous. It's her relentless efforts that continue to inspire generations.

5. Kittur Chennamma

Led an armed rebellion against the East India Company [23rd Oct 1778 - 21st Feb 1829]

Kittur was born on 23rd Oct 1778, in Kakati, a small village in Karnataka, India. She received training in horse riding, sword fighting and archery at a young age.

As a princely state rebel queen, Kittur Chennamma remains an icon of the Indian Independence Movement and Rani of the Kittur, a former princely state in Karnataka. Rani Chennamma was the first woman independence activist of India who had stood against the British Empire all alone. Kittur did not succeed in driving them away, but she did provoke many women to rise against the British rule. She is best known for her leadership in an armed rebellion against the East India Company. She did not give up come what may and was arrested. She passed away in imprisonment.

Since then, Rani Chennamma has become a legend. During the freedom movement, her brave resistance to British formed the theme of several plays, songs and song stories.

6. Vijay Laxmi Pandit

The first woman (and the first Indian) president of the United Nations General Assembly [18th August 1900 - 1st December 1990]

Vijay Laxmi Pandit was born on 18th August in Allahabad to Motilal Nehru and Swarup Rani Nehru. Motilal Nehru was a politician, national leader and a wealthy barrister who served twice as a president of the Indian National Congress. She was the sister of India's first Prime Minister Jawaharlal Nehru.

Vijay Laxmi played an active role in India's Freedom Movement and was imprisoned by the Britishers on three different occasions in 1932 – 1933, 1940 and 1942 - 1943. She also led India's delegation to the

General Assembly in 1947, 1948, 1952 and 1963. She was appointed as India's first ambassador to the Soviet Union in 1947. Early in 1949, she became Ambassador to the United States. She was the first woman to hold a cabinet post. She was an Indian Ambassador for Russia during the late forties and later, the Governor of Maharashtra. Pandit is best known for being the first woman President of the UN General Assembly. She also served as India's first representative to the United Nations Human Rights Commission in 1978.

She was the member Aligarh Muslim University Executive Council but never received any formal education. Pandit's own writings include 'So I Became A Minister' (1939) and 'Prison Days' (1946). Pandit died in Dehradun, India on December 1st 1990.

On her death anniversary in 1990, President Rama Swami Venkataraman described Pandit as a "Luminous Strand in the tapestry of India's freedom struggle. Distinctive in her elegance, courage and dedication, Mrs Pandit was an asset to the National Movement."

Her contribution to India is something that the country can never forget.

7. Anandi Gopal Joshi

The first female doctor of India [31st March 1865 – 26th Feb 1887]

Anandi Gopal Joshi was considered as the first female doctor in India. She was born in Kalyan in the Thane, Mumbai district on March 31st 1865 in Maharashtra. She was the first Indian woman who was trained in western medicine and the first woman to travel to the United States of America.

Following the pressure from her family and the conservative traditions of that time, Anandi was married at a young age of nine to Gopal Rao Joshi. It was he who helped Anandi receive an education in Medicine.

Anandi, with the encouragement and motivation gained from her husband, applied to the Women's Medical College of Pennsylvania. She travelled to New York by ship. She began her medical training at the age of 19. Due to cold weather and an unfamiliar diet, her health deteriorated in America. She suffered from Tuberculosis. Despite her bad health, she stayed motivated to complete her MD in medicine. Her journey to get an education was so inspiring; she gained much publicity in the Indian press on her graduation in Medicine so much so that the Queen of England Queen Victoria also congratulated her. She had created history by becoming the first woman of Indian origin to study and graduate with a degree in medicine in the United States. Anandi became an inspiration for future women generations to pursue higher education.

On returning to India in 1886, after completion of Medicine in the US, she received a grand welcome by the Indian government and was appointed as a Physician-in-charge at the Albert Edward Hospital in Kolhapur [in present-day Maharashtra].

Just a month before her 22nd birthday, on February 26th 1887, Anandi Gopal Joshi died of tuberculosis, which left the whole nation in grief. The entire nation mourned her death, and it made headlines across Indian media. Her dream of establishing her own medical college was left unfulfilled.

The Institute for Research and Documentation in Social Sciences (IRDS), an NGO from Lucknow, presents the 'AnandiBai Joshi Award for Medicine' in honour of her early contribution to Medical Science in India. Fellowship in the name of Anandi Gopal was also established by the government of Maharashtra.

8. Sarojini Naidu

The Nightingale of India [13th Feb 1879 – 2nd March 1949]

Sarojini Naidu was born in Hyderabad in an educated Brahmin family. She was the eldest daughter of Aghorenath Chattopadhyay, who was a scientist, philosopher and educator. He was also the Principal of Nizam College Hyderabad. Her mother Varada Sundari Devi was a poetess in the Bengali language.

Sarojini Naidu too was a great poetess, an Indian freedom activist and politician. She earned the sobriquet of the 'Nightingale of India' or 'Bharati Kokila'. Her political activities and role in the freedom struggle led her to imprisonment in 1930, 1932 and 1942 for 21 months.

Sarojini Naidu as a child showed excellent performance in academics and was attracted to poetry. She was proficient in different languages which included English, Urdu, Telugu, Bengali and Persian. She topped her matriculation exam from Madras University. She impressed all by applying her literary skills. She wrote a 1300-lines-long poem in an English title 'The Lady of the Lake'. A few months later, Sarojini wrote 'Maher Muneer' in the Persian language. Impressed with her work, the Nizam of Hyderabad granted her a scholarship to study abroad. At the age of 16, she got admission in the King's College, England and later joined Girton College in Cambridge.

After the independence of India, she became the first Governor of the United Provinces (now Uttar Pradesh) and retained this role till her death in 1949.

Through poems, this Nightingale of India expressed all her feelings, emotions and personal experiences and became an incredible poetess of the 20th century. In 1905, her first collection of poems was published under the name of 'The Golden Threshold'. Later, in 1961, Padmaja Naidu, the daughter of Sarojini Naidu, further published her second collection of poems named 'The feather of the Dawn'. In 1925, Naidu became the President of the Indian National Congress. Her birthday is honoured as Women's Day all over India.

Naidu may have died on 2nd March 1949 due to a cardiac arrest in her office at Lucknow, Uttar Pradesh, but she has continued to remain alive in our hearts forever through her contribution to Indian poetry.

Most of her work was transformed into songs. Her inspiration was the beauty of nature and the Indian contemporary life events. Her poetry echoed with the ethos of her patriotism.

She lived a glorious life by her own words,

"As long as I have life, as long as blood flows through this arm of mine, I shall not leave the cause of freedom.... I am only a woman, only a poet. But as a woman, I give you the weapon of faith and courage and the shield of fortitude. And as a poet, I fling out the banner of song and sound, and bugle call to battle. How shall I kindle the flame which shall waken you men from slavery...." -- Sarojini Naidu.

9. Mother Teresa

The first Indian woman to win a Nobel Prize [26th August 1910 – 5th September 1997]

As a nun and selfless missionary, Mother Teresa devoted her life to serving the poor, orphans, disabled, aged, sick and destitute around the world. She was canonised by the Roman Catholic Church as the 'Saint Teresa of Calcutta.' Mother Teressa was born in Macedonia to parents of an Albanian- descent. Having taught for 17 years, Mother Teresa felt a "call within a call" in 1946.

She was given permission to join a group of nuns in Ireland when she was only 18. After a few months of training, she arrived in India and began working as a teacher. However, she ended up starting the "Missionaries of Charity" due to widespread poverty in Calcutta. The Missionary now has branches throughout the world.

In 1952, Mother Terresa established the first home for dying, where people can die with dignity. She spent all her time with those who were dying and made the neglected people feel that there was someone who cared for them.

She established a hospice, centres for blind, aged and disabled, and homes for orphans and abandoned children. In 1957, she began to work with lepers (those suffering from leprosy, a terrible infectious disease). She led an enormous scale of charitable activities and touched millions of lives until her dying day.

Mother Teressa suffered various health problems over the last two decades of her life, but nothing could stop her from fulfilling her mission of serving the poor and needy. She held only the most humble conception of her own achievements. Mother Teresa was the founder of the Missionaries of Charity, a Roman Catholic congregation of women dedicated to helping the sick and poor.

She is considered as one of the 20th century's greatest humanitarians, who received the Nobel Prize in 1979.

From: No Greater Love

"It is not how much we do, but how much love we put in the doing. It is not how much we give, but how much we put in the giving." - Mother Teressa.

10. Captain Prem Mathur

The first woman pilot in India [born on 17th January 1910]

Prem Mathur was born on 17th January 1924 in Aligarh, Uttar Pradesh. Her desire of becoming a pilot was associated with her determination, courage, resilience, strength and hard work. This an ambitious and passionate lady could see her dream come true and got an aviation pilot licence when she was just 21-years-old. Captain Prem Mathur, a young girl hailing from Allahabad, dared to create history by becoming the first Indian woman commercial pilot and started flying for the Deccan Airway. She obtained her pilot's license in 1947. In 1949, she won the National Air Race.

Piety, domesticity, submissiveness, all which are considered signs of true femininity, were challenged by Captain Mathur. She illustrated that women are equally capable of engaging in intellectual pursuits and are no way inferior to men.

11. Indira Gandhi

The first woman Prime Minister of India - The Iron Woman of India [19th November 1917 – 31st October 1984]

Indira Priyadarshini Gandhi was born on 19th November 1917 in Allahabad and was the only daughter of Kamala and Pt. Jawaharlal Nehru. Smt. Gandhi actively participated in the freedom struggle. She was a great Indian politician, political leader and a central figure of the Indian National Congress. She was the first and, to date, the only female Prime Minister of India. She served as a Prime Minister from January 1966 to March 1977 and again from January 1980 until her assassination in October 1984, becoming the second longest-serving Indian Prime Minister, after her father Jawaharlal Nehru.

Political intransigency and unprecedented centralization of power were the qualities of Prime Minister Indra Gandhi. In support of the independence movement, PM Gandhi went to the war of independence in East Pakistan, which resulted in an Indian victory and the creation of Bangladesh, as well as an increase in India's influence to the point where it became the regional hegemon of South Asia.

PM Gandhi was presented with the highest civilian honour award, the Bharat Ratna after leading India to victory against Pakistan in the Bangladesh liberation war in 1971.

On 31st October 1984 as a revenge of the Golden Temple assault, Indira Gandhi was assassinated by her own bodyguards and Sikh Nationalists at her residence at Safdarjung Road in New Delhi.

"Woman of the Millennium" was the honorary name given to PM Indra Gandhi in an online poll organized by the BBC.

12. Prathibha Patil

The first woman President of India – [Born on December 19th 1934]

Prathiba Patil was born on 19th December 1934 in Nandgaon, Jalgaon district of Maharashtra, India. Prathiba Devisingh Patil is an Indian politician who served as the 12th President of India from 2007 – 2012. A member of the Indian National Congress, Patil was the only woman to hold the office. In 1967, Prathiba Patil became the first Deputy Minister for Education. In 1985, she was elected to the Rajya Sabha as a Congress candidate and served as the 24th Governor of Rajasthan from 2004 – 2007.

Prathiba Patil along with her husband established an educational institution called "Vidya Bharati Shikshan Prasarak Mandal", which operates a chain of schools and colleges in Jalgaon, Mumbai, Delhi and Pune. She also established an Engineering college and an Industrial Training School for the visually challenged along with several schools for poor children.

13. Kiran Bedi

The first woman to join the Indian Police Services – [Born on 9th June 1949]

Kiran Bedi was born in Amritsar on 9th June 1949. She is a retired Indian police officer, social activist, former tennis player, politician and the current Lieutenant Governor of Puducherry. She played an instrumental role in introducing the Prison Reform in India. She was the first woman to join the Indian Police Services and remained in service for 35 years before taking voluntary retirement in 2007 as the Director-General, Bureau of Police Research and Development.

Her education included an undergraduate degree in English in 1968, a master's degree in political science in 1970, a Law degree in 1988, and a PhD in social science in 1993 with a focus on drug abuse and domestic violence.

In 2005, CUNY School of Law awarded her an honorary Doctorate of Law degree in recognition of her "humanitarian approach to prison reforms and policing."

She further received the 1999 Serge Sotiroff Memorial Award for her outstanding contribution to international drug control efforts by the Navjyoti Delhi Police Foundation

She was also conferred with Acharya Tulsi Kartritva Puraskar in 2005 by Akhil Bharatiya Terapanth Mahila Mandal.

14. Bachendri Pal

The first Indian woman to scale Mount Everest – [Born on 24th May 1954]

Bachendri Pal is an Indian mountaineer, who became the first Indian woman to reach the summit of Mount Everest in 1984. She was presented with Padma Bhushan, the third-highest civilian award by the Government of India in 2019.

Pal is the founder and director of the Tata Steel Adventure Foundation in Jamshedpur and has guided more than 4,500 women on numerous mountain expeditions.

Advising women, Pal says, "I always tell women that there is nothing they cannot achieve. Conquer your inner Everest first and then no mountain will be unscalable."

Pal nurtured the institute. She led the all-women expeditions in 1993, 1994, and 1997 which eventually created seven world records and set benchmarks for Indian mountaineering.

Pal admits, "For me, my journey to Everest symbolized women's empowerment. It was an awakening of my abilities. In the end, the choice is yours — to stop or keep pursuing."

15. Indra Nooyi

One of the most powerful women in the business world - [Born in 1954]

Indra Nooyi [Krishna Murthy] was born to Tamil Parents in 1955 in Madras, India [Chennai]. After receiving her Bachelor's degree in Physics, Chemistry and Mathematics in 1974 from University of Madras, she did her Post Graduation Program Diploma from Indian Institute of Management Calcutta in 1976. Later, Nooyi moved to the USA in 1978 and earned a Master's Degree in Public and Private Management in 1980.

Indra's success from Chennai to IIM Kolkata to Yale and to the Head and CEO of Multinational cooperation is inspiring. Nooyi started her career as product Manager at Johnson and Johnson. Later on, she joined PepsiCo. in 1994, and was named CEO in 2006. She also lead divestiture of Tricon, now named as Yum! Brands; it includes companies like Pizza Hut, KFC, Taco Bell under its umbrella. In 1988, Nooyi also took the lead in acquisition of Tropicana and with Quaker Oats Company. At present, Nooyi is serving as a member of the Board of Directors at Amazon, and the International Cricket Council and Schlumberger.

Nooyi's dedication, commitment and leadership abilities made her stand at the top in the list of most powerful women in the world. Nooyi was named one of the "Best CEOs in the World" by the CEOWORLD Magazine in 2018. Forbes magazine ranked Indra Nooyi on the 2008 through 2017 lists of The World's 100 Most Powerful Women. She was also ranked #1 by Fortune Magazine in its annual ranking of "Most Powerful Women in Business" for 2006, 2007, 2008, 2009 and 2010.

Indra Nooyi was named one of the "Greatest Global Living Legends" by NDTV. On 14th December 2013, she was awarded by the President of India Pranab Mukharjee at the Rashtrapati Bhavan.

Nooyi was honoured by many prestigious awards which includes Padma Bhushan by the President of India in 2007.

Indra Nooyi is an inspiring woman who battled against turbulent times, conquered odds and etched a mark in history, the kind of success women can achieve. She acknowledged the constraints and challenges women face to acquire positions of Power.

"I see the struggles women go through, and you cannot expect every woman to be superwoman. It just does not work because there is one constraint we all have, and that is that there are only 24 hours in a day." - Indra Nooyi.

Indian business women like Indra Nooyi, Shaika Sharma, Zia Mody, Swati Piramal, Anu Aga, Chanda Khochar, Sulajja Firodia, and Naina Lal have put India in an enviable position in the Globe.

"The challenge of a leader is looking around the corner..and making the change before it's too late to make the change…" — Indra Nooyi

16. Kalpana Chawla

The first woman of Indian origin to reach the space – [March 17th 1962 – 1st February 2003]

Kalpana Chawla was not only the first woman of Indian origin but also the first American astronaut to reach space. Till date, she is fondly remembered by the world for her exceptional achievements and success in this field. However, on 1st February 2003, she died in a space shuttle accident in Columbia. Chawla was among the seven astronauts who met with the disaster while coming back to the Earth. The remains of the crew were scattered at the National Park in Utah.

To honour her bravery and achievements, the first satellite of Met – Sat series, "MetSat-1" launched by India was renamed as Kalpana-1. Kalpana was also posthumously awarded the Congressional Space Medal of Honor.

17. P.V. Sindhu

The first Indian woman to win the BWF (Badminton World Federation) Championship. [born on 5th July 1995]

Pusarlavenkata Sindhu was born in Hyderabad on 5th July 1995. Both her parents PV Ramana and Vijaya, were national-level volleyball players. Sindhu started playing badminton at the age of eight herself. She got her first major recognition by coming fifth in the All India ranking championship under 10 categories. She then won the doubles title at the sub-junior Nationals and during the all India ranking Puna under 13 categories. She further won the gold medal in the under 14 categories at the 51st National School Games in India.

P V Sindhu, eventually, became the first Indian to win the BWF World Championship. She is additionally among the only two Indian badminton players to ever win an Olympic medal — the other one being Saina Nehwal. She is also the first Indian woman to win a silver medal in the Olympics 2016. She then won the silver medal in women's singles in 2018 too.

Arjuna Award was bestowed to Sindhu for Badminton on 24th September 2013.

Padma Shri Award, the fourth highest civilian award in India, was awarded to Sindhu in March 2015 along with a Rajiv Gandhi Khel Ratna Award, the highest sporting honour of India, on 29th August 2016.

18. Pranjal Patil

The first visually impaired IAS officer [born on 1st April 1988]

Pranjal Patil is India's first visually impaired IAS officer who cracked the UPSC entrance exam in 2015.

Pranjal was born on 1st April 1988 in Wadaji Village Jalgaon, Maharashtra. She was born with a poor vision. At the age of six,

Pranjal lost her complete vision and was endowed with 100% blindness. However, she was a very bright student. She pursued Master of Arts (MA), Master of Philosophy (MPhil) and then PhD in International Relations.

With the help of a technology named Job Access With Speech (JAWS), a screen reading software, Pranjal began preparing for the UPSC entrance exam. The one who tries never loses and she was resilient enough to know this. Hence, as India's first-ever visually impaired female IAS officer, Pranjal Patil proved it right by clearing India's toughest exam twice in a row. Pranjal attempted the UPSC entrance exam in 2015 for the first time, cracked it with AIR (All India Rank) 773 and was then qualified for the UPSC in the second attempt with AIR 124. It was a big achievement for her. She became the first blind student to be qualified for IAS and was admired throughout the nation.

On 14th October 2019, Pranjal took charge as the Sub-Collector of Thiruvananthapuram.

During an interview, she stated -

"Success doesn't give inspiration; the struggle behind success gives you the inspiration. But success is important because only then people will be interested to know your struggle. The attitude and the approach to do something matters and each individual can become a building block for a beautiful society."

While assuming charge, Pranjal said, "We should never be defeated and we should never give up. With our efforts, all of us will get that one breakthrough which we want."

A GREAT FEMINIST ENGLISH WRITER IN WORLD HISTORY

VIRGINIA WOOLF [25th January 1882 - 28th March 1941]

Virginia Woolf was born in South Kensington, London, United Kingdom. Her mother, Julia Prinsep Jackson, was a pre- Raphaelite artist's model, while her father Sir Leslie Stephen was a famous scholar and philosopher. Virginia Woolf was homeschooled in English Classics and Victorian Literature, as in those days, it was a tradition to send only the male child for a college education. Woolf is considered as the most important novelist, critic, modernist and feminist writer of the twentieth century. Woolf wrote 10 novels and a number of nonfiction books. Her writings include essays on politics of war, artistic theory, literary theory and women writing. She used the Stream of Consciousness as a narrative device which focuses more on the character's inner thought than on the plot. Her writings can be best described as impressionistic, a literary style which rather than recreating reality, inspires impressions. Apart from her writings, she was successful in her educational reforms too.

Virginia's early life during summers was spent in St. Ives, Cornwall, where she first saw the Godrevy Lighthouse, which later became central in her novel 'To the Lighthouse' (1927).

Then came an abrupt end to Woolf's childhood at the age of 13 with the death of her mother in 1895. That's when she suffered her first mental breakdown. Woolf started writing professionally in 1900 with encouragement from her father. However, she suffered another mental breakdown in 1905 when her father passed away as well.

Virginia married Leonard Woolf, a brilliant young writer and critic from Cambridge, England in 1912. The couple established the Hogarth Press in 1917, wherein much of her work was published. Her work gained much attention for inspiring feminism. Woolf was noticed as a key figure of the 1970s for Feminist criticism. 'A Room Of One's Own' in 1929 is regarded as the basic beginning text of feminist criticism, which attracted a lot of attention. Presently, she is given a special place in women's studies programs for her pioneering feminism.

Virginia Woolf 's major achievements include her novels: Mrs. Dalloway, To the Lighthouse and Jacob's Room (1922). The Voyage Out (1915) first brought her critical attention. Night and Day (1919) is traditional in the method. The Short Stories of Monday or Tuesday (1921) brought critical praise towards her way. In the Waves (1931), she masterfully employed the stream of consciousness literary technique which stresses 'free writing'. Other novels include Orlando (1928), The Years (1937), and Between the Acts (1941).

Throughout her life, Virginia Woolf suffered from mental illnesses and went through breakdowns after her parents' deaths. Even then, her illness and suffering did not affect her productive work of writing. She carved her name in the world of English Literature with her exemplary writings.

"The history of men's opposition to women's emancipation is more interesting perhaps than the story of that emancipation itself."

- Virginia Woolf

~~~~~~~~~~~~~~~
~~~~~~~~~~~~~~~

BARRIERS TO GIRLS EDUCATION

A keen observation reveals many factors that are barriers to girls' education. It is a sad truth that these barriers are created by the society and people themselves, but great women have proved that they have the ability to overcome all the barriers and marked their success in every walk of life. A few of these barriers are:

- Illiteracy of parents
- Poverty
- Child labour
- Unavailability of resources
- Transport problems
- Lack of sanitation for girls during menses
- Health issues
- Lack of support and guidance

- Lack of motivation and inspiration to learn
- Gender discrimination
- Cultural norms and expectations
- Stereotypes
- Household duties and domesticity
- Subservience
- Lack of social consciousness among women
- Co-education
- Lack of qualified female teachers
- Poor infrastructure
- Early marriages and pregnancy
- Conflicts and crisis
- Insecurity and unsafe environment
- Sexual harassment
- Trafficking
- Assaults and injustice with women
- Extremism
- Patriarchal system of society
- Government reforms
- Poor political will and conviction

To point out the reality of a typical Indian society that is the root cause and an important factor for women or girls' illiteracy is the illiteracy, unemployment and poverty of parents. Generally, uneducated parents are least concerned about the education of their children, especially daughters. They instead, come up with innumerable cultural norms and expectations from daughters by imposing household responsibilities on them. Education is given least importance or no importance at all. In most of the traditional societies, it is observed that getting daughters married at the earliest is the aim of a parent's life. This mindset forces children into child marriages or early marriages. Uneducated girls are obviously chosen by uneducated or least educated men, who cannot afford to provide them with the basic needs of life. This is when the conflicts begin. Men who are incapable of handling the responsibilities of their family emerge as a violent, impolite, unkind, irresponsible and dominant character. With this, future generations continue to suffer and get spoiled. Domestic violence, insecurity, sexual harassment, gender discrimination continue and lead to failed, unsuccessful, poor, unhealthy, uneducated, economically backward family structure and patriarchal system of society.

Lack of resources like transport facilities for girls and women, secure and safe environment, proper sanitation, cleanliness, female teachers, social consciousness, motivation to learn, guidance and support from family and many more factors have become major barriers to women's education too. Extremist religious groups stop women from seeing their dreams turn into reality. Social and cultural norms also play a major role in hindering women from getting their education. Apart from all these barriers, a major influence of political will and conviction is observed. There is no political will to overcome inequality and gender discrimination. Despite many schemes and policies implemented by the government of India, poor execution is key for the lack of education to girls and empowerment of women. Most of these schemes are beyond the reach of common uneducated and underpowered women.

This reality prompted me to take up the topic of girls' education and women empowerment. In this current scenario, it becomes our fundamental duty and right to convert these barriers into opportunities and resources for girls' education. After so many years of gaining independence, women and girls in India are still under the clutches of many barriers. The government has a significant role to play. The government must take the necessary steps for providing free education and creating employment opportunities. Parents must be given awareness about the importance of girls' education and the consequences of not educating their daughters through social media and different campaigns. The government must provide all the needed resources like safety measures, safe and secure environment, transport facilities, better sanitation, regular health checkup, fitness programs, immense importance to health and hygiene, extra and co-curricular activities, life skills seminars and workshops, counselling and guidance for girl students. Awareness against child sexual and physical abuse must also be spread in schools in order to protect girls from sexual predators. When girls are enabled to protect themselves, the biggest challenges in their lives become easier. It can be achieved through dedicated and trained teachers.

A survey has reached a point that women make great teachers because they are gentle, kind and possess abilities to understand children far better than men. Children find them more helpful and caring as teachers. Women play a vital role in educating girls, especially adolescents. Girls and their parents feel more comfortable with women as teachers. Lack of female teachers stop parents from sending their daughters to school in most of the rural areas. Lack of female teachers also has proved to be a big barrier for girls' education. In order to overcome this barrier, the government needs to take strong steps to make it easy for girls to reach higher education by providing girls with different resources like easy, safe and convenient transport facilities for schools,colleges and universities. Financial assistance must be provided at every stage to educate and empower women for making the best teachers out of them. Teachers' training programs, seminars and workshops must be conducted to prepare teachers for upcoming challenges. Best teachers can bring a great change through their skills of motivation and inspiration, which ignites a thirst in their students to get educated and bring revolution in our society. Teachers must be continuously appreciated and awarded for their excellent contribution towards making responsible citizens of the nation.

"To call woman the weaker sex is liable; it is man's injustice to woman. If by strength is meant moral power, then woman is immeasurably man superior."

M. K. Gandhi
(Mahatma, Vol. 3, P. 33)

~~~~~~~~~~~~~~
~~~~~~~~~~~~~~

GOVERNMENT INITIATIVES FOR WOMEN EDUCATION AND EMPOWERMENT IN INDIA

In order to uplift, educate and empower girls and women in India, the government has launched schemes and taken certain steps to provide reservations for women in the public and private sectors. Here is a list of such schemes and women empowerment initiatives.

National Policy On Education [1968]

NPE is formulated by the Government of India to promote education - from elementary to college level. It is focused on providing educational facilities to all the citizens of India. The principles formulated for the development of education include free and compulsory education, education for teachers, language development, education opportunities for all and uniform educational structure. Major emphasis is laid on women's education. Gender injustice with respect to educational access is also recognized. Vocational, technical and professional education is made available for women empowerment.

Mahila Samakhya Program [1988]

The New Education Policy of 1968 compelled the launch of MSP in 1988 for the empowerment of rural women belonging to the socio-economically weaker sections of the society. With over 21,000 villages under this scheme, the program directed at providing educational provision as well as raising awareness via seminars and meetings. It provides a space for rural women to meet, discuss issues, gain general knowledge and awareness. It aims at enhancing self-esteem, intellectual abilities and self- confidence of women. It helps recognize the contribution of women to the society, polity and economy. It is an effective tool for women empowerment.

Nari Shakti Puraskar aka Women Power Award [1999]

Nari Shakti Puraskar was first awarded by the Government of India in 1999. It is India's highest civilian award for rendering distinguished services and efforts for the cause of women. This national-level award was presented by the President of India on 8th March on International Women's Day at Rashtrapati Bhavan in New Delhi.

Sarva Shiksha Abhiyan – [2001]

This scheme is equipped with the purpose of providing education to children between 6 to 14 years. It aims at the universalisation of primary education. This is centred basically on women with a deprived background. Padhae Bharat Badhae Bharat is a nationwide subprogram of SSA.

National Program for Education of Girls at Elementary Level - [2003] NPEGEL

Girls who are not initiated through the Sarva Shiksha Abhiyan are covered by NPEGEL. This scheme has covered around 24 states to institute model schools to provide better opportunities for the education of girls in India. It is aimed at reaching the "Hardest to Reach" girls, especially those who are not in schools

The 86th Constitutional Amendment Act [2004]

It is a cracking initiative towards the implementation of women education in India. This act stated elementary education as a fundamental right for children aged between 6 to 14 years.

Kasturba Gandhi Balika Vidyalaya Scheme - KGBV [2004]

It aims at the establishment of Upper Primary Residential Schools for girls. It basically works in rural areas where female literacy is low. Schools are set up as a part of this scheme, with 100% reservations – 75% for backward classes and 25% for below poverty line girls.

Sakshar Bharat Mission for Female Literacy [2008]

It aims at promoting women education under which Lok Shiksha Kendras were set up.

Saakshar Bharat Mission [8th September 2009]

This mission was launched with an objective to cut down the women illiteracy rate in the country. It aims to impart functional literacy to non-literates in the age bracket of 15 to 35. It aims to promote the dream of Education for All.

SABLA – Rajiv Gandhi Scheme for Empowerment of Adolescent Girls [1st April 2011]

It aims to address the multi-dimensional problems of adolescent girls which include nutrition and health education, life skills education, vocational training, child care, home management, family welfare, health checkup and referral services. This program covers adolescent girls between 11 to 14 years of age.

Beti Bachao, Beti Padhao [22nd January 2015]

This campaign is aimed at the eradication of female foeticide and awareness towards the education and welfare of girls, especially in rural areas of India. It aims to ensure the protection of the girl child and also helps to improve the efficiency of the welfare services for girls. It ensures the participation of girls in various fields too.

One-stop Centre Scheme [1st April 2015]

It aims to set up One-Stop Centres that are funded by the Nirbhaya Fund and receive financial assistance from the Central government. It aims to support and assist women affected by violence at public or private places irrespective of their caste, gender, religion, region or marital status.

Women Helpline Schemes [1st April 2015]

The purpose of the schemes is to provide a 24-hours immediate response to women affected by sexual harassment, sexual offence, violence at public and private places.

Swadhar Greh - [2015]

This scheme is envisioned for the rehabilitation of women in difficult circumstances. The Swadhar Scheme was launched by the Union Minister of Women and Child Development in 2002. Under this scheme, women and girls are provided with shelter, food, clothing, medical treatment and care for women who are in need. It also enables women to regain emotional strength lost due to unfortunate circumstances. Swadhar Greh helps depressed women start life afresh with dignity by supporting them economically and emotionally. The beneficiaries include widows deserted by their families and relatives, women prisoners released from jail and without family support, women survivors of natural disasters, women victims of terrorists, extremists, domestic violence, trafficked women and women affected by HIV/AIDS who do not have any social and economical support.

Mahila – E – Haat [7th March 2016]

The Ministry Of Women And Child Development has launched a direct online marketing platform. This is a part of digital India's initiatives to support women entrepreneurs, self-help groups [SHGs] and non-governmental organizations [NGOs] to showcase the products and services rendered by them. Women can market their products by registering themselves at www.mahilahaat.rmk.gov.in

Mahila Shakti Kendra [2017]

Mahila Shakti Kendra was launched by the government of India in 2017 for the empowerment of rural women. It aims at skills development, employment, digital literacy, health and nutrition. It works at the national, state and district levels. Currently, this scheme has started working in almost 115 backward districts.

Working Women Hostel Scheme [6th April 2017]

This scheme is supervised by the Women and Child Care Ministry Govt of India. It was launched on 6th April 2017. Under this scheme, safe and conveniently located accommodation for working women along with daycare facilities for children is provided. Employment opportunities are also provided. The main objective is to empower women. Widowed, single, separated, physically handicapped, below poverty level women and female trainees are also allowed to opt for this scheme.

Moreover, there are mid-day meal programs and free distribution of uniforms and books for girls, etc. Still, one has to work towards certain matters such as transport facilities, infrastructure, teacher and student ratio, the safety of female children at school, better curriculum, and sanitation facilities so that more and more girls can be educated. Furthermore, parents must accept the importance of education without discriminating between male and female children. There are many more miles to go to eradicate gender inequality. Hence, one must accept the fact that an educated woman is capable enough to perform all her roles with greater responsibility than an uneducated one.

Every member of the society must confidently take the necessary steps to educate girls and women regardless of their religion, tradition, culture and beliefs.

Philosophy of education may differ in every religion according to its rules and principles, but every religion does give basic rights of education irrespective of one's gender.

"No country can ever truly flourish if it stifles the potential of its women and deprives itself of the contributions of half of its citizens."

—Malala Yousufzai

~~~~~~~~~~~~~~~
~~~~~~~~~~~~~~~

CONCLUSION

This research was done and published with a simple yet profound vision that every person who reads it gets an undistorted perspective of the importance of women education. It is an attempt to erase the misconception of education of women in Islam. The study has shed light on the contribution of outstanding women, who had authority, who had skills, who had struggled hard for the upliftment of the society, who challenged the entrenched patriarchal system in society, who created a path for women to come out of the supposedly superior male-dominated spheres, who changed the overall perspective of the world, who brought a great revolution and who are responsible for the progress of today's women - they bear the crown of our growth and success. They were the ones who were respected in their own time by society. It is time one must stop reacting to the existence of such great women as shocking, uncommon, unusual or perhaps surprising. Sometimes, such women broke the norms to such an extent that they were not even mentioned by their contemporaries.

Today, women ought to learn from the instances and qualities of such great women in history. The only way women, in general, could pay respects to their sacrifices, struggles, courage, pain and sufferings is by being inspired enough to remain brave and courageous in the face of tyranny and patience in the times of trouble. The lives of these great successful personalities have taught us that through trials in our lives, one gains success and through success, life gains beauty. This beauty becomes our identity and one leaves an unerasable mark in the society through a spirit of motivation for the future generations.

"Never be afraid of falls; every fall will make you rise stronger than before."

- Sara Hassan [author]

These great personalities have proved through their lives that disabilities, rejections, failures, tough times or life challenges couldn't stop them to fight for their dreams. They have set examples for the youth worldwide to work hard with the best of their capabilities. It is true that one's will power and belief takes a person to his/her ultimate dream. It is extremely important for us to empower ourselves without the assistance of others because self-confidence and realization of self-worth is the basis of achieving all that one wants.

The progress of the society and the country lies in the upliftment of women. This is possible only when women enjoy the right to control and get benefits from the resources, assets, income and their own time, as well as to manage risk and challenges and improve their economic status and well-being.

The social transformation of women is an essential element in national development. Since women constitute more than half of the population, there can be no development unless the needs and interests of women are taken into account. In fact, transformed women are a nation's strength.

A woman's social transformation can become a reality through conscious efforts and this is possible only through combined efforts of many factors in society.

- The first factor is in the mind of the woman and how she should not prioritize social expectations over her aspirations and dreams. Ambitions are not to be concealed; they are to be strived for and achieved.
- Society should change its attitude towards women's aspirations and dreams. Transformation of the family, society, nation and the whole world is possible only through the inborn qualities of women.
- Awareness must be created regarding the importance of women education and the outcomes of educating girls and women in society.
- The true and the correct teachings of Islam must be taught and encouraged to erase the misconceptions and wrong interpretations of Quranic verses and hadith for educating women.
- Women must take responsibility for their own education and education of female children.
- The government must stop targeting and discriminating any particular religion like Islam. The consequences will be worse for the government to face as this will directly affect the development of the whole nation in general and women's empowerment and education in particular.
- The government must take necessary steps to uplift and empower women and create awareness through awareness programs, seminars, workshops, campaigns and other activities.
- Life skills and soft skills programs must be conducted for psychological growth and development of qualitative criteria like self-confidence, self-esteem, ability to take decisions and freedom of expression. This helps in overcoming psychological issues like stress, depression, anxiety, etc. and leads to the improvement of the overall health of womankind.
- At many instances, the government of India has failed to provide security and safety to girls and women. Girls have been becoming victims of sexual violence. Despite implementing several programs and schemes for the safety of women, daughters of India feel unsafe at every place they live in. Hence, the main responsibility of the government is to provide women with high security so that they can live in a peaceful and secured environment.

- A healthy, peaceful and safe environment promotes academic achievements along with overall development of individuals. Every member at home, society, community and nation must take responsibility to provide a secured environment to women for them to give their best.
- Women must be provided with efficient resources to get educated and empowered. In every field seats must be reserved and no discrimination must be made on the basis of caste, tribe or religion. Women can polish their hidden capabilities and can come out with flying colors when provided with best opportunities.
- The economic damage caused by Covid-19 is now widely acknowledged globally as well as for India. Dealing with the after-effect of Covid-19 will be a major challenge over the next few years to prevent long term economic disaster. Among many policy actions taken up by government of India, education and empowerment of women cannot be neglected as this is the basis of a country's growth and prosperity.
- Unemployment has increased unexpectedly due to pandemic outbreak. Lockdown, isolation and quarantine has restricted people at home resulting in great demand for online business. Most of the people from rural areas and many in urban places are not aware of digital marketing and business. Government and social organizations must provide free classes and seminars to help people learn and understand digital world.
- The recovery from Covid-19 crisis must lead to a higher economy than ever before. It is possible only by strong focus on building more equal, inclusive and sustainable economies and societies that are more resilient in the face of pandemic and other global and social challenges irrespective of caste, tribe, religion, region and gender.
- Solidarity is the need of today's world. With solidarity we can defeat Corona and other challenges to build a better world.

~~~~~~~~~~~~~~
~~~~~~~~~~~~~~

ABOUT THE AUTHOR

[MS. SARA HASSAN]

Sara is a native of the Telangana state of India. She started her education from Islamia Model High School in Yakutpura, Hyderabad at a very young age of two. Her father Mr. Khaja Hassan and mother Mrs. Jaweeda Begum are founders of the Islamia Group of Educational Institutions in Hyderabad. From the very early years in her life, Sara was inspired by her parents' work. For her, they are true examples of dedication, cooperation, sacrifice, and hard work. Her parents have given her practical examples by the establishment of Educational Institutions.

The journey of education was challenging at a certain stage for Ms. Hassan as she faced strong opposition in continuing her education, but her determination in her goal was to see herself as a highly educated person who can become a motivation and inspiration for girls and women. According to her, **"No force and no hurdle can stop a woman who is determined to see her dreams come true. This is only the matter of her own hard work, dedication and sincerity to her aim."**

She completed her intermediate studies and then graduated from Hyderabad's Osmania University. Lack of support and encouragement could not become a barrier in her path, rather she used them as positive challenges to reach the highest level. Her determination to her basic, human, social and economical rights was firm. Bearing many setbacks, she was awarded Bachelor of Education in 2000, followed by Master in Arts (English Literature) and then PGCTE and then MEd (Master in Education) in 2017. She is now pursuing a PhD in Education.

Sara has proved her abilities and talents by teaching students from nearly fourteen different Nationalities which include students from Saudi Arabia, Kuwait, Egypt, Sudan, Yemen, Syria, Jordan, Indonesia, Lebanon, Palestine, Philippines, Bangladesh, Pakistan and India from 2006 to 2011. She worked as an English Lecturer and Exam Committee Chair in the English language department, University of Hail, Kingdom of Saudi Arabia from 2012 to 2015. She received many awards and honours like Employ Of The Month, Employ Of The Year, Certificates Of Appreciation, Certificates Of Achievement and many more during her work.

She has conducted many workshops and seminars for the professional development of educators, teachers, lecturers and principals at different educational institutions which were highly appreciated. Life skills workshops and programs conducted by her for students, teachers and parents benefitted amazingly.

Though Hassan is not a National or International visionary symbol, she stands to represent a common Muslim woman of today's world. Her unseen and unrecognized struggle makes her voice echo through this research work.

"Women are the strongest part of society who can bring a change, let our voice echo, let us create a vision, let us bring revolution and make history."

- Sara Hassan [author]

~~~~~~~~~~~~~~
~~~~~~~~~~~~~~

REFERENCES

- Raza, Moonis (1990): Education, Development and Society, New Delhi
- Sopher, D.E (1980): "Sex Disparity in Indian Literacy", in Sopher (ed.) An exploration of India: Geographical Perspective on society and culture, New York
- Rae, Sambasive G, Ed (1979): Problems of Women's literacy, Mysore; Central Institute of Indian Languages.
- Aktherul Wasey (1977): Education of Indian MUSLIMS: A study of the All India Muslim Educational Conference (1866-1947), New Delhi: Asia International
- Arnold, T and A. Guillaumme (1931): The Legacy of Islam, London.
- Bhattacharya, S (2001): Education of women in India, New Delhi: Kanishka Publishers

- Roy, S (1979): Status of Muslim Women in North India, New Delhi
- Rustogi, P. (2003): Gender Biases and Discrimination Against Women: What do different indications say?
- UNESCO, 2006, The Impact of Women Teachers on Girls' Education, Bangkok: UNESCO
- Lake, L. 2015. "The Silver Bullet: Girls' education as the entry point for systemic change". Forthcoming place: Camfed.
- ICRW (International Center for Research on Women).2006. Child Marriage and Domestic Violence. Washington, DC: International Centre for Research on Women.
- Lerner, Gerda (1986). The Creation of Patriarchy, Women and History. Oxford University Press, pp. 8-11. ISBN
- Macionis, John J (2012). Sociology (13th ed.) Prentice-Hall.
- Shahida Lateef (1990): Muslim women in India, New Delhi, Kali for Women.
- Siddiqui, H.Y(1951): Muslim Women in Tansition, New Delhi
- Ahmed, Imtiyaz Ed. (1981) "Muslim Educational Backwardness: An inferential Analysis"
- Dr. Annie Jhon S.V Shindi, "Educational status of Muslim Women in India."
- "Education and gender equality" UNESCO. 25 April 2013. Retrieved 15 October 2018.
- Human Development Data (1990-2017) Human Development Reports. Retrieved 15th October 2018
- Indicators of Gender Equality in Education - OECD Retrieved 15th October 2018
- M. Abul Fadi, "The saying of the Prophet Muhammad (pbuh)", No. 424
- Syed Sajjad Husain and Ashraf, S.A (1979): Crisis on Muslim Education, Jeddah King Abdul Aziz University

- Mernissi, F (1993) "The forgotten queens of Islam."
- Nadwi, Mohammad Akram (2013) Al Muhaddihat: the women scholars in Islam.
- Bader, Clarisse (2001) Women in Ancient India
- Kashif-ul-Huda (6 May 2007) "Genetically Indian: Story of Indian Muslims" Radiance views weekly. Retrieved 18 March 2011.
- "Indian Families" Facts about India. Archived from the original
- Verma, Suman, Saraswati, T.S. (2002). Adolescence in India. July 22, 2013
- Raman, Sita Anantha (2009). Women in India: A Social and Cultural History.
- Parihar, Lalitha Dhar (2011) Women and law: from improvement to empowerment.
- Basu Aparna (1991) "Women' s History in India, A Historiographical Survey."
- Katty Kay and Claire Shipman - "The confidence code"
- Women and Education in Islam - Minhaj ul-Quran
- Majumdar, R.C (2014): Great women of India, Kolkata: 2014, Swami Madhavananda, Ramesh Chandra Majumdar
- Joshi, Rama, Liddle, Joanna (1986), Daughters of independence: gender, caste, and class in India.
- Forbes, Geraldine (1999), Women in modern India, Cambridge University Press, A major scholarly survey.
- Basu, Aparna (1991), "Women's History in India: A Historical Survey"
- Rao, R.K (2001) "Women and Education", Kalpaz Publication, Delhi
- Agarwal S.P (2001), Women Education in India: Present status, Perspectives, Plan, Statistical indicators with Global view," Concept Publications co. New Delhi, Vol 3, NO. 5

- Esere, MO (2001) "Women empowerment and its challenges to gender counselling," Journal of counselling and Human Development, Vol.1, No. 1, pp. 16-31
- Mosedale, Sarah (2005) "Assessing Women's empowerment towards a conceptual framework." Journal of International Development.
- Salim Al Hassani, Women's Contribution to Classical Islamic Civilization: Science, Medicine and Politics
- Arafat Jan, Rufaida Al Asalamiya, the First Muslim Nurse, Journal of Nursing Scholarship
- Omar Hasan Kasule, Sr, Historical Roots of the Nursing Profession in Islam
- "United Nations: Gender equality and women's empowerment" United Nations Sustainable Development.
- Oxfam, "Women's Economic Empowerment Conceptual Framework."
- Castle Stephen, 'Social transformation and Globalization,' CAPSTRANS Development, 2000.
- Abd Allah Ahmed Naim (2008). Islam and the Secular State: Negotiating the Future of Shari'a Havard University Press. P 161.
- Yogesh Atal (2009) Sociology and Social Anthropology in India. Pearson Education India
- Barazangi, Nimat Hafez. Woman's Identity and the Qur'an: A New Reading. Gainesville, Lla: University Press of Florida, 2004.
- Barlas, Asma, "Beliving Women" in Islam: Unreading Patriarchal Interpretations of the Qur'an. Austin: University of Taxis Press, 2002.
- Levy, Reuben (1999), The Social Structure of Islam. London: Routledge

- Jouseph, Suad, Najmabadi, Afsaneh (2005) Encyclopedia of Women and Islamic Culture.Leiden: Brill
- Detail interpretation of Quran: Ibn Kaseer
- Tafseer ul Quran by Al Moudidi
- Detail study of Hadees Al Buqari
- Detail study of Hadees Al Muslim
- Al- Baghdadi, Ibn Saad, Tabaqat Vol VIII, P.92 -93
- Nomani, P. 259-60
- “Great Women of Islam”- by Dar- us - Salam Publications
- Abdul Ahad Darrusalam, The Honorable wives of the Prophet (Publishing Info, 2004) 79-82
- Ahmad Thompson, The wives of the Prophet: Umm Salamah.
- Tafseer Nomani Vol 27, P.374
- Sahih Al Bukhari, 4: 56: 819
- Al- Bukhari, Muhammad, Sahih Al Bukhari Book 4,5 8
- Ibn Hisham, Abdul Malik(1955)
- Al- Serah Al- Nabaweyah
- Ibn Kathir’s Al Bidayah wa -An- Nihayah
- ‘Amazing Women Scholars’, The true Knowledge. Retrieved 2 March 2015.
- Nadwi, Mohammad Akram (2007). AL.Muhaddithat: the women scholars in Islam. London: Interface Publishers.
- https://en.m.wikipedia.org
- www.isdb.org
- www.culturalindia.net
- www.knowindia.gov.in
- www.journals.sas.ac.uk
- www.yourstory.com

- www.carrierride.com
- www.dw.com
- https://d1.islamhouse.com
- www.goodreads.com
- www.beliefnet.com
- www.dar-us-salam.com
- www.whyislam.org
- www.brainbuxa.com
- www.questia.com
- www.firstpost.com
- https://theculturetrip.com
- www.womenweb.in
- www.learnreligion.com
- www.aliaslam.org
- www.iosrjournals.org
- www.mastercard.us
- www.encounteringislam.org
- www.researchgate.net
- https://eric.ed.gov
- www.theguardian.com
- www.api-gbv.org
- www.youthkiawaz.com
- www.nios.ac.inn
- www.bbc.com
- www.indiafolks.com
- www.bloomberg.com
- www.ncbi.nlm.nib.gov

- www.tandfonline.com
- www.thoughtco.com
- womennow.in
- www.unfpa.org
- sustainabledevelopment.un.org
- wcd.nic.in
- www.weforum.org
- www.worldvision.org
- en.m.wikipedia.org
- www.bsr.org
- knowindia.gov.in.
- www.huffpost.com
- www.equalityhumanrights.com
- www.ohchr.org
- www.humanrights.com
- shodhganga.inflibnet.ac.in
- https://Quran.com
- www.islamicstudies.inf

~~~~~~~~~~~~~~
~~~~~~~~~~~~~~

I will be waiting here.......
For your silence to break,
For your soul to shake,
For your love to wake!

Jalal Uddin Rumi
13th Century